Front endpaper Early morning visitors to Heian Shrine peek through the massive vermilion doors as shrine priests within perform their morning tasks.

Page 1 Offerings of *sake* and fresh vegetables are presented on high trays to the gods at Hirano Shrine. Even today, shrine priests, while performing Shinto rites, are garbed in clothing and clogs modeled on those of the ancient court.

KYOTO
CITY OF ZEN

VISITING THE HERITAGE SITES OF JAPAN'S ANCIENT CAPITAL

Judith Clancy

Photography by Ben Simmons

TUTTLE Publishing

Tokyo | Rutland, Vermont | Singapore

CONTENTS

Pages 2–3 The poise and grace of Gion's young *kimono*-draped *maiko* (apprentice *geiko*) extend down to their gleaming white *tabi* socks in raised wooden *geta* footwear.

This page, anticlockwise from top Snowy accents on a lion's head. Summer visitors enter a *noren*-curtained entrance for a tea ceremony. A black-lacquered window frames the glorious autumn scenery of Kyoto. Traffic-streaked lights shimmer below the World Heritage pagoda of Toji Temple. Too good a chance to pass up, a visitor attempts to capture a temple's resident tabby. A lusciously glazed tea bowl is presented to a guest.

CHAPTER 1

INTRODUCING
KYOTO

Kyoto

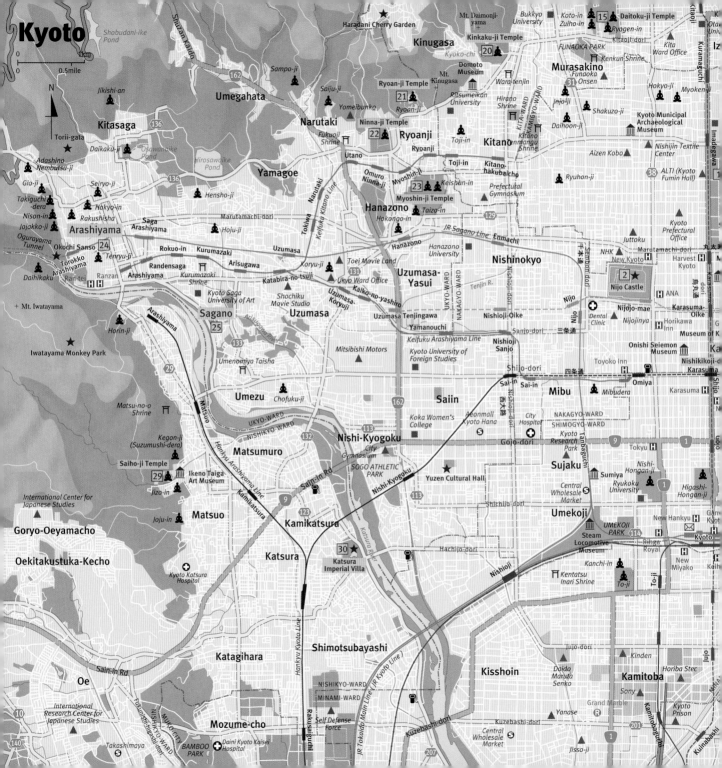

0 1km
0 0.5mile

Shobudani-ike Pond
Jikishi-an
Kitasaga
136
Adashino Nembutsu-ji
Gio-ji
Takiguchi-dera
Nison-in
Jojakko-ji
Ogurayama Tunnel
Arashiyama
24
Okochi Sanso
Torokko Arashiyama
Daihikaku
Mt. Iwatayama
Horin-ji
Iwatayama Monkey Park
29
Matsu-no-o Shrine
Kegon-ji (Suzumushi-dera)
Saiho-ji Temple
29
Ikeno Taiga Art Museum
Jizo-in
Joju-in
Matsuo
International Center for Japanese Studies
Goryo-Oeyamacho
Oekitakustuka-Kecho
Kyoto Katsura Hospital
10
International Research Center for Japanese Studies
140
Oe
Mozume-cho
Takashimaya
Daini Kyoto Kaisei Hospital
BAMBOO PARK

Shuzan Kaido
162
Sampo-ji
Saiju-ji
Yomeibunko
Fukuoji Shrine
Seiryo-ji
Hokyo-in
Rakushisha
Saga Arashiyama
Hensho-ji
Hoju-ji
Daikaku-ji
Osawanoike Pond
Hirosawaike Pond
136
Yamagoe
Umegahata
Umehata
Haradani Cherry Garden
Kinugasa
Mt. Daimonji-yama
Kinkaku-ji Temple
20
Ryoan-ji Temple
21
Ryoanji
22
Ninna-ji Temple
Narutaki
Utano
Omuro Ninna-ji
Myoshin-in
23
Keishun-in
Hanazono
Hokongo-in
Taizo-in
Myoshin-ji Temple
129
Tokiwa
Narutaki
Keifuku Kitano Line
Marutamachi-dori
Rokuo-in
Kurumazaki
Uzumasa
Koryu-ji
Randensaga
Kurumazaki Shrine
Katabira-no-tsuji
Arisugawa
Kaiko-no-yashiro
Toei Movie Land
Ukyo Ward Office
Uzumasa-Koryuji
Uzumasa-Yasui
Uzumasa Tenjingawa
Yamanouchi
Hanazono University
Mitsubishi Motors
Kyoto Saga University of Art
Shochiku Movie Studio
Sagano
25
Arashiyama
133
131
Koka Women's College
Aeonmall Kyoto Hana
Kyoto University of Foreign Studies
Nishikyogoku
City Gymnasium
113
Nishi-Kyogoku
SOGO ATHLETIC PARK
Yuzen Cultural Hall
113
Umenomiya Taisha
Umezu
Chofuku-ji
162
Saiin
Sai-in
Sai-in
Mibu
Mibudera
Koka
NAKAGYO-WARD
SHIMOGYO-WARD
Kyoto Research Park
Sujaku
Central Wholesale Market
Ryukoku University
Sumiya
Nishi-Hongan-ji
Higashi-Hongan-ji
Umekoji
UMEKOJI PARK
114
Steam Locomotive Museum
Kanchi-in
Kentatsu Inari Shrine
To-ji
To-ji
Nishioji
Matsumuro
Matsuo
Kamikatsura
123
Katsura
30
Katsura Imperial Villa
Hachijo-dori
Kyoto Katsura Hospital
9
Sain-in Rd
Kamikatsura
Kamitoba
Kisshoin
Shimotsubayashi
Katagihara
Sain-in Rd
207
201

Ritsumeikan University
Domoto Museum
Mt. Kinugasa
Ryoan-ji
Wara-tenjin
Hirano Shrine
Kitano Tenmangu Shrine
Kitano
Kitano-hakubaicho
Toji-in
Prefectural Gymnasium
Ryuhon-ji
Nishinokyo
NHK
New Kyoto
2
Nijo Castle
Nijo
Dental Clinic
Nijojo-mae
Nijojinya
Nishioji-Oike
Sanjo-dori
Nishioji Sanjo
Onishi Seiemon Museum
Toyoko Inn
Shijo-dori
Omiya
Karasuma

Bukkyo University
Koto-in Zuiho-in
15
Daitoku-ji Temple
Ryogen-in
FUNAOKA PARK
Kenkun Shrine
Kita Ward Office
Murasakino
31
Funaoka Onsen
Jinjo-ji
Daihoon-ji
Shakuzo-ji
Hokyo-ji
Myoken-ji
Kyoto Municipal Archaeological Museum
Aizen Kobo
Nishijin Textile Center
38
ALTI (Kyoto Fumin Hall)
Juttoku
Kyoto Prefectural Office
Marutamachi-dori
Harvest Kyoto
ANA
Karasuma-Oike
Horikawa Inn
Museum of Ky
Nishikikoji-d
Karasuma
Tokyu
9
1
Nishi-Hongan-ji
1
New Hankyu
Rihga Royal
New Miyako
Kyoto
Jujo-dori
Kinden
Horiba Stec
Daido Maruta Senko
Sony
Grand Marble
Central Wholesale Market
Jisso-ji
Kyoto Prison
Kamitoba
1
Kuinabashi-dori

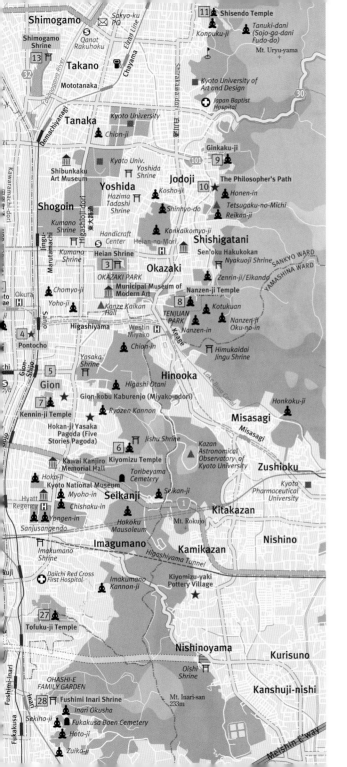

KYOTO'S MAIN HERITAGE SIGHTS

*See district maps on pages 66 (Northern Kyoto), 96 (Western Kyoto) and 122 (Southern Kyoto) for sites outside this map.

PREVIOUS SPREAD Below a calendar depicting the garden within, a pair of modest *zori* thong footwear sit on a shelf in a temple's entrance.

INTRODUCING KYOTO

For thousands of years, footsteps have smoothed this land. First barefooted, then wrapped in straw or raised on wooden clogs, feet continue to pat down mountain trails and river banks, divide orderly rows of vegetables, meander through stately gardens, mount temple steps, thread alleyways and stroll along concrete sidewalks. The feet that strode these passageways span centuries, encompassing tradition and modernity. Today, feet shod in sneakers,

Above left Framed within cinnabar red shrine gates, a Shinto priest in formal headgear and silk robes invokes the resident gods of Yoshida Jinja, a shrine founded in 859.
Left The sun casts a long elegant silhouette on a stone-inlaid lane in the Miyagawa *geiko* district.
Right Beautifully attired in colorful summer cotton *yukata*, young women gather before Kyokochi Mirror Pond at the Golden Pavilion. A World Heritage Site, the estate became a Buddhist temple in 1422, but the stroll garden surrounding the pond and pavilion remains much as it was 1,000 years ago when property of a court aristocrat.

children's shoes sporting cartoon characters, British oxfords and Italian stilettos, or *kimono*-clad citizens in elegant *zori*, impart their signature tone and tempo to the city.

The home of seventeen World Heritage Sites, over a thousand temples and shrines and some of the world's most beautiful gardens, Kyoto now resonates with the footfall of appreciative tourists.

Above left Raised stepping-stones in the garden of Okochi Sanso entrancingly lead one to the rustic, yet elegant Tekisui-an teahouse on the estate of the late film star, Okochi Denjiro (1898–1962). The stones are deliberately spaced to slow the visitor in the approach to the teahouse, allowing one to savor the scenery. The infinity-shaped pathways farther on lead to a garden the actor designed for meditation.
Left Toyokeya, a neighborhood *tofu* and *yuba* shop, located near Kitano Shrine.

Top A traditional *toro* stone lantern stands at the edge of the garden pond (with a reflection of the wooden five-storied pagoda) amidst autumn foliage at Toji Temple, a World Heritage Site.
Above The vast gravel courtyard fronts the immense Founder's Hall (Goei-do) of Higashi Hongan-ji temple in the vicinity of Kyoto Station. Founded in 1602, it is one of two head temples for the Jodo Shinshu Sect of Pure Land Buddhism. The building supports a roof of 175,000 clay tiles making it one of the world's largest wooden structures.

A BRIEF HISTORY OF JAPAN'S ANCIENT CAPITAL

The city of Kyoto began to take shape in the 8th century when some of its earliest residents, the Hata family, invited the Emperor to make his home on their hunting grounds. Under the most rigorous dictates of geomancy, planners created a grid of roads patterned after the western Chinese city of Xi'an, terminus of the Silk Road.

Rich with game, traversed by rivers and sheltered on three sides by mountains, Kyoto began its transformation into one of the great cities of the 9th century. By the late 800s, the network of avenues and byways had become the new Imperial Capital. Workers who lived in rough huts helped build a palace and estates for the nobility. A political court thrived on ritual, bureaucratic intrigue, poetry and the newly introduced spiritual practices of Buddhism, a faith introduced to the former court in Nara.

Molded by deep religious beliefs and rent by warring factions, Kyoto began its journey through history, not only as an imperial stronghold but also as a vibrant residential city, with enclaves of astute merchants, gifted artisans and hard-working commoners who lived alongside the temples, shrines and gardens that even today stand as tributes to the skills and ancient aesthetics of their creators. But as much as Kyoto is rich with remnants of a remarkable past, it is a forward-looking city, as embodied in the architecturally stunning and massive Kyoto Station.

Kyoto is also a city festooned with ugly electric wires and burdened with lumpish apartment buildings, intrusive sidewalk notices and gaudy neon signs. Discarded bicycles lie in gnarled mounds. For while Kyoto residents are truly proud of their city and its historic artistic legacy, some have perfected enough selective vision to overlook aesthetic insults.

Some would say that it was a series of historical accidents that allowed Kyoto to become one of the world's metropolitan jewels. Other would argue that it could have been no other way. In 1868, after the Meiji Restoration, the Emperor and his court, as well as the heads of prestigious families, moved from Kyoto to the new capital of Tokyo, then a collection of rural towns known as Edo. Despite fear that losing its status as the capital would pitch Kyoto into decline, it thrived. The city is not only a stronghold of tradition but early on embraced progress. In 1890, it built one of the country's first large-scale engineering feats, a canal that allowed rice from the agricultural prefecture of Shiga to be shipped efficiently into the city. Kyoto also quickly established hydroelectric power, realigned streets to allow construction of a railroad station and boasted the country's first tramcar.

The members of the oldest families who remained behind founded Nintendo, Kyocera, Murata Manufacturing and Shimadzu Corporation, now among some of the world's leading companies, while Kyoto University boasts of Nobel Prize recipients in chemistry and physics.

Top left The top-knotted head of a warrior bowing to the Emperor.
Left The Imperial chrysanthemum motif on a gate at Shoren-in Temple.
Top The blossoming of spring along the Eastern Mountains.
Above The straw sandal shod feet of Kukai, the 9th century monk who founded the Shingon sect of Buddhism in Japan.
Right Young musicians aboard the magnificent Naginata Float during the Gion Festival.

Above center A literary tradition of poetry writing outings was one of the pleasures of the 10th century Heian court, as depicted in this painting of nobles seated along a meandering stream.
Top Tiger motif walls.
Above Painting of courtiers on horseback.
Left Stone image of a demonic figure supporting a great weight.

ZEN
BUDDHISM
AND THE TEA CEREMONY

Zen was the last Buddhist sect to enter Japan, and by the 14th century one that had a profound influence on the arts: calligraphy, Noh drama, architecture and especially the tea ceremony.

Zen is based on meditation, a practice in which one looks into the source of the mind, leading to an inner equilibrium between the secular and the sacred and, hopefully, enlightenment. Some claim that Zen is more a discipline or philosophy than a religion, but 1,500 years of Zen writings reveal it to be one of the world's great spiritual traditions. Unlike conventional religion, with a transcendent deity outside of the self, Zen believes that the essence of mind is innately enlightened, and that seeing into one's Buddha nature is possible through meditation. It was largely as an aid to meditation and good health that Eisai, the Japanese monk who introduced Zen to Japan, brought tea seeds back with him from China and

Left The wall of a Buddhist monastery hung with straw hats and sandals.
Below left Neatly placed footwear rests in a temple entrance of pleasingly symmetrical lines of wood, stone and tile.

promoted the drinking of tea. Use of the beverage spread quickly among the priesthood and the ruling classes.

After being taken up by the aristocracy, the drink became a privilege of a rising wealthy class. In the late 16th century, the tea master, Sen-no-Rikyu, started to refine the art of making tea into a ceremony, stipulating that all who entered his teahouse were equals to share in the pleasure of a simple bowl of whisked powdered green tea. This was a revolutionary idea, since Japanese society was rigidly

Opposite A Buddhist/mendicant monk awaits alms from passersby.
Above Two dragons, one clutching the sacred jewel in its five claws, soar through the vaporous mists on the high ceiling of a Buddhist temple, Kennin-ji.
Left Monks standing in repose before being received into a temple.

Top left Preparation for a winter tea ceremony begins with setting the iron kettle into a sunken hearth.

Top center A tea master carefully ladles hot water into a soft-fired Raku tea bowl.

Above A guest closes the *shoji* paper window set within a black-lacquered cusped frame in this tea ceremony room. Ornamentation is kept to a minimum, with a hanging scroll in the alcove and a single seasonal bud.

Right With an outstretched palm, a guest receives the whisked green tea from a *kimono*-clad hostess.

class-bound. Thereafter, the tea-room became a meeting ground for priests, artisans, merchants and aristocrats, a singularly powerful cultural statement.

Perhaps this is one reason that Toyotomi Hideyoshi, a common foot soldier who rose to the rank of warlord, was attracted to the tea of Sen-no-Rikyu. The warlord became a patron of this famous tea master, recognizing Rikyu's influence on society and his undisputed ability to create new aesthetic standards. Artists were inspired to create utensils that embodied these aesthetics, and tea enthusiasts vied in collecting new pieces. During one military excursion in the 16th century, Hideyoshi invaded Korea and brought back Korean potters to reproduce the simple rice bowls

that are still highly sought after. Imparting the softness of human touch, the bowls rested lightly in two hands, their thick walls warming but not scalding. Sen-no-Rikyu recognized beauty in bowls shaped by an expert eye and glazed in soft tones—the pinnacle of graceful simplicity. The Japanese eye has become trained to recognize rustic beauty (*wabi*), elegant simplicity (*sabi*), understated tastefulness (*shibui*) and vague mysteriousness (*yugen*), a deep response to the passing of beauty (*aware*) or refined sophistication (*miyabi*), as a few examples of the many expressions still in the aesthetic lexicon that concern tea utensils.

Consequently, most teahouses have rustic settings. Some even have thatched roofs and all have

simple unadorned clay walls, a hearth or hanging kettle, an alcove for a hanging scroll, a simple flower arrangement and *tatami* mats. For Japanese to slip through the low door, sit quietly while listening to the low hiss of the kettle sounding like the wind through the pine trees, is a return to the heart of their culture, a respite from the demands of modern life and its interruptions. It is a journey back to their cultural identity.

Left The shadows of autumn reflect on a single bowl of powdered green tea resting on *tatami* flooring.
Below Red felt carpeting offers a bit of warmth to winter visitors in this temple. The sweet is first consumed, followed by a sip of slightly bitter powdered green tea.

KYOTO'S AMAZING ARCHITECTURAL HERITAGE

Japan's indigenous *kami*, or gods, live not inside shrines but within the towering cypress trees, sacred springs and waterfalls that surround the buildings. There, in nature, devotees can stand in the spiritual presence of the gods while seeking favor and guidance. The simplicity of a Shinto shrine never competes with its natural setting.

Under Shintoism, Japanese have stood in awe of the power and beauty of nature and the religion's simple shrines embody this reverence. The *torii* that identifies a shrine entrance is often construct-

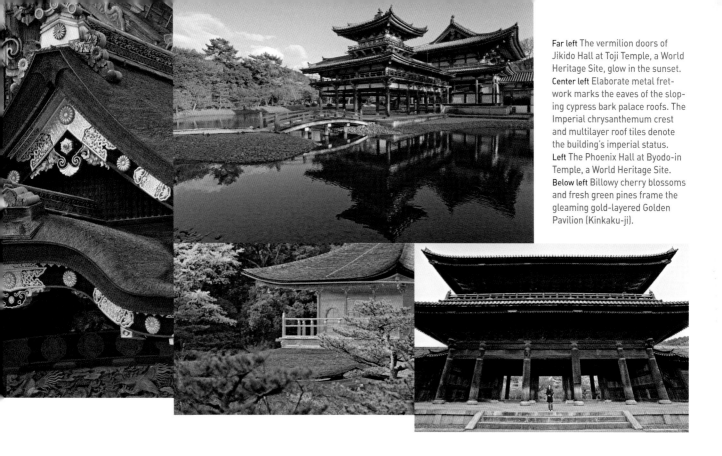

ed by four pieces of timber. These gates invite those closest to the gods, their feathery messengers the birds, to sit on the crossbeams, ready to wing supplicants' prayers heavenward.

Temples are an entirely different affair. When Buddhism arrived in Japan in the 6th century, Japan, still without an alphabet, relied on written Chinese to convey the tenets of religion, law and philosophy. Scholars, diplomats and artisans were invited to the Nara court (60 kilometers away) to impart a culture distinctly different from—and admired as superior to—Japan's. With its sophisticated philosophy and texts, Buddhism immediately appealed to Japan's courtiers who controlled the privilege of literacy, but the religion rapidly reached even illiterate peasants and merchants.

The Chinese adaptation of the Indian religion brought new dimensions of the understanding of the universe and life beyond this one. This new theology was not grounded in the immensity of a cypress tree or the roar of a waterfall. It demanded human-made artifacts: a written text, a myriad of implements, statuary and, grandest of all, huge structures to accommodate believers.

By 596, temple construction had begun. Chinese carpenters were invited to Nara and introduced their techniques to a wonderstruck population. The temples we see today in Kyoto, although fairly faithful descendants of Japan's 6th–10th century originals, differ greatly from those still in existence in China. Japan's climate and earthquake-prone land made

Top A late afternoon visitor poses under the gigantic gate of Nanzen-ji Temple.
Above Walls are works of art as well as enclosures. The layered earthen clay is interlaced with flat tile work inset with a single rounded tile.

Below The iconic face of Kyoto streets is its townhouse (*machiya*). In keeping with neighborhood expectations, Starbucks has opened a branch in a renovated old *machiya* along the cobblestone slope of Ninenzaka.
Bottom A feline resident of the Pontocho *geiko* district seeks entry into a typical townhouse characterized by a wooden lattice (*koshi*) frontage, curved bamboo fencing (*inuyarai*), clay rooftiles aligned in a one-stroke design (*ichimonji*), and short curtain (*noren*) that indicates that the shop is open for business, perhaps even furry ones?

Bottom right Many traditional old homes still exist in the southeastern district of Daigo. Late afternoon sun imbues the wooden structure with warmth.

elevated buildings a necessity. Its rich supply of zelkova, cypress, oak and cedar forests lent itself to increasingly mammoth worship halls as the population embraced the comfort of salvation within a Buddhist paradise.

Not only did places of worship begin to be shaped in Kyoto, but some of the world's greatest collections of Buddhist images are found here. One of Asia's most iconic forms, the pagoda, continues to pierce the ancient skyline, serving as a reliquary for Buddha's remains and as a revered landmark for Kyoto residents.

Abundant forests have long provided Kyoto with wood to build massive temples and the houses of commoners' alike. The understated beauty that defines the Kyoto townhouse, the *machiya*, owes much to its reliance on wood, with its rich palette of hues and variety of grains, which residents lovingly buff until the surface gleams. The glow of well-cared-for wood is enhanced by the plaster and earth that form the *machiya* walls, the paper windows that shield inhabitants from cold, and the woven straw *tatami* mats that cover most floors.

Much of the present-day iconic design of these townhouses dates from the great Temmei Fire of 1788. The devastation and the

need to quickly rebuild huge swathes of the city led to a uniformity of style that has left its imprint on the city.

The architectural layout of most of the inner-city houses features slatted lattice fronts; open clay "windows"; an inner garden; and

Below In keeping with its commitment to preserving local architecture in the vicinity of Kiyomizu-dera temple, Starbucks kept some traditional elements such as a raised *tatami*-mat area with cushioned seating at low tables and paper sliding windows that suffuse the interior with a soft comfortable light, while also providing chairs in another area.

a long, narrow kitchen with an overhead skylight to admit light and disperse smoke. The curved bamboo fencing along the roadside wall adds an aesthetic element that cloaks its practical function: it once protected the outer clay walls from damage by spoked cart wheels.

It is no wonder that passersby find the exteriors—the dark-stained wooden fronts, quiet sliding entry doors, and undulating tile roofs—visually soothing. Today, however, because so many *machiya* are being refashioned into shops, galleries, and restaurants, visitors can also glimpse the inner environments that shaped lives with the quality of their

space, texture, and soft light—features that reflect the warm, human sensuality of an organic structure.

Right A flowering potted plum bonsai is an inviting addition to Kimata, a well-appointed traditional inn and restaurant of fine cuisine. The added features of bamboo blinds (*sudare*) and stone lantern (*toro*) bespeak of its reputation for hospitality and traditional elegance.

Below right The famed designer, Issey Miyake, opened a shop in a 132-yr-old *machiya* townhouse located on Yanaginobanba Street in central Kyoto. The simple lean lines of the traditional architecture and attractive courtyard garden complement the design sense of the clothing line within.

UNIQUE KYOTO FOOD TRADITIONS

Traditional Japanese cuisine, especially that of Kyoto, is one of the most sophisticated food cultures in the world. Kyoto's rich food culture dates back a thousand years, with today's chefs drawing on centuries-old records detailing ingredients and techniques. Specialized food for the old Imperial court and, later, wealthy merchants, was presented, as it still is today, in bite-sized pieces easily handled with chopsticks. Often served cold, it was accompanied by a hot soup and rice.

The fields of Kyoto boast several distinct vegetables, collectively called *kyo-yasai*. Kyotoites are very familiar with their local produce, and accord it a place of honor in exclusive restaurants and in the homes of discerning epicures.

The soy product *tofu* is a Kyoto specialty. It is made by soaking dried beans overnight in good quality well water, churning them into a smooth mash, straining and then boiling the resulting soy milk, and adding calcium sulfate to act as a

coagulant. The mixture is then poured into block molds to set.

Tofu adopts itself to a variety of dishes. Smooth silky *tofu* (*kinu*) is served cold in summer with a dab of grated ginger. A firmer type, *momen*, is often cut into cubes, simmered in a kelp broth, and then scooped out and dipped into a light soy-flavored sauce. In addition to plain *tofu*, many of Kyoto's supermarkets as well as the food courts found in the basements of department stores sell *tofu* flavored with

sesame seeds, black beans or *shiso* (perilla).

Another unique Kyoto soy-based food product is *yuba*, the film formed on the surface of boiled soy milk. The thin, translucent beige sheets are hung, and then sold dried or fresh. The taste is a delicate, slightly sweet concentrate of soy milk. *Yuba* accompanies many a Kyoto dish, especially in the multi-course *kaiseki* meal served in better restaurants.

Although it is the gourmet epitome of Kyoto cuisine, *kaiseki* grew out of the simple meal served at a formal tea ceremony. The present-day *kaiseki* meal developed in the 16th–17th centuries as the merchant class gained wealth and sought out rarified ingredients and preparations to impress prospective clients.

While delicious, *kaiseki's* most striking characteristic, however, is what meets the eye. *Moritsuke*, the artistic arrangement of food, is an art form in itself, and the dishes on which the food is served are a critical component. For example, the chef will consider color and texture and perhaps even reference the food to flowers or poetry. Presentation is so highly regarded that diners often whip out their cell phones to photograph the dish before them, perhaps to show their friends or to relish in memory the anticipation of culinary pleasure—before a single taste! Then comes the pleasure of uncovering the different dishes as one would unwrap a present, each course a delight to both eye and palette, each a culinary gift.

Top Multi-courses of elaborately presented meals are served on a selection of ceramic dishes, lacquered bowls and sometimes leaves, making the meal as visually pleasing as it is a culinary delight.
Above Blowfish (*fugu*) is as expensive as it is occasionally lethal. Chefs must be specially licensed to serve this delicacy, for the liver, when improperly prepared, can be highly toxic.

KYOTO'S EXQUISITE ARTS AND

CRAFTS

This page Home to the court for 1,000 years, the city attracted its most talented artisans who continue to produce the highly prized crafts of Kyoto. Lacquered paper umbrellas, painted doors backed with gold foil, handcrafted paper-covered tea canisters, paper fans of seasonal motifs and a gorgeously glazed array of dishes produced in the Kiyomizu area along the Eastern Hills, reveal the refinement of its artisans.

The variety of arts and crafts available to Kyoto residents, the fruit of generations of artists and ateliers, is truly splendid. Surprisingly, the best place to survey the breathe and width of crafts is a department store, notably one of the larger ones: Takashimaya, Daimaru and Fujii Daimaru. The sixth floors are reserved for crafts: lacquer ware, metal utensils, ceramics, bamboo and wooden items, *kimono* and all manner of woven and dyed items. Exhibition halls and galleries are also an integral part of the stores as are the restaurants on the seventh floors, making department stores mammoth reservoirs of social, culinary and cultural activity, in addition to their primary commercial role.

There are numerous craftspeople practicing their art in the city today, most notably *kimono* and *obi* sashes,

for rarely does a single person design and make one item. Most are collective enterprises that span many ages and skills. The Nishijin district is filled with businesses that import raw silk, begin the process of dyeing it, encase some threads with gold or silver foil for the *obi*, sell and repair looms, operate spinning machines, specialize in threading looms—all leading to the production of clothing—and the wholesellers who line Muromachi Street offering magnificent seasonal showings of their products, for *kimono* and *obi* are not mass produced; each is custom designed and made.

Just saying the word "Nishijin" conjures up resplendent images of elegant wear, but the original meaning of the word denotes the Western campsite of a decade-long war. The rivers in Kyoto might be one of the reasons the weaving and dyeing industry settled here, for the Kamo River was often the site of luxurious lengths of dyed silk being washed and readied for the next stage of work. Today, most looms are automatic Jacquard looms, but individual artists still dot the area, especially the fingernail weavers, who spend hours bent over the cloths patiently straightening the weft with serrated fingernails, and the *obi* weavers, who create unique designs either for wealthy clients or performing artists.

Another famous product is *Kiyomizu-yaki*, ceramics made near the Kiyomizu Temple. Today, the old wood-firing kilns are not allowed in the city, and most production takes place in a ward beyond the Eastern Mountains. Using centuries-old techniques, steady hands apply delicate tendrils of gold enamel glaze before loading the pots into kilns for their last firing. Many shops and galleries along the Eastern Hills (Higashiyama) display fine porcelain and clay products, often with high prices that reflect the work and talent that went into them.

The best-known crafts shop is the Kyoto Handicraft Center, west of Higashi-oji, on Marutamachi-dori. Items range from simple greeting cards to high-end antiques with a nice representation of woodblock prints, cloisonné, pearls, lacquerware and swords.

Many antique and print shops and galleries are clustered along Nawate-dori, Furumonzen-dori and Shinmonzen-dori, three areas north of Shijo, near the Shinmachi and Gion districts, and along Teramachi, north of Sanjo-dori. A stroll along these streets can be like visiting a museum, but one in which you are allowed to handle the exhibits.

The best artists in the land served the court, and even today the concentration of ateliers makes Kyoto a delight for those with a discerning eye.

Top Many steps are necessary in producing a *kimono*. This woman is shading a stretched length of silk to be dyed, one of the early steps in the process.
Above left The art of wearing a *kimono* involves understanding motifs and color combinations, the dictates of the social status of the wearer and the demands of the occasion. Here, a model pivots on the runway during one of the *kimono* shows that are featured daily at the Nishijin Textile Center.
Above A busy employee in the textile center answers a customer's question.
Left A fragrant branch of the blossoming daphne infuses the tearoom with spring.

Above Decades of experience are needed to become a master weaver: an understanding of the textures and colors of the threads to be selected, along with the technical dexterity of managing all the spindles and shuttles involved in producing a single *obi*. Right An exquisite array of dyed silk skeins fills several walls at Kawamura Weavers in Nishijin.

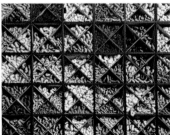

Top Katsuji Yamade applies hot liquid wax to a length of silk hung across his studio and held in place with bamboo stays. He will decorate the entire length before the cloth is sent to the steamers for fixing the dyes and then to a seamstress for assembly.
Above A careful selection of colored silk is readied to bring to the loom.

KYOTO'S AMAZING FESTIVALS

As the men lift a one-ton portable shrine unto their shoulders, they cry out "Hoitto, hoitto" to announce that local gods are on their way. There are few places in the world where communities celebrate festivals as enthusiastically as in Kyoto. These impressive events have evolved into gorgeous pageants laden with cultural richness. Embodied in the festivals' aesthetic element, is the serious business of appeasing and pleasing the myriad Japanese gods who love to be entertained by their descendants, the Japanese people, who in turn love to celebrate their deities.

Festival time brings a variety of customs that are synchronized in the cultural heart of Kyotoites. Families display treasured heirlooms and offer charms to dispel ill health. Gods are moved from their home shrine to a smaller more distant one. Massive portable shrines are jostled on the shoulders of men, exuberantly shouting *hoitto hoitto* or solemnly pulled through the capital streets to the musical accompaniment of transverse flutes and bells. Their path is aflutter with *kimono* sleeves, while sky-high halberts

sway in the air above.

The Gion Festival, one the city's oldest, is now designated an intangible World Heritage. This mid-summer extravaganza culminates in two solemn processions on July 17 and 24. Other activities such as assembling the floats, practicing *gion-bayashi* music, selecting participants, and preparing offerings all require community effort. Households in each district contribute money for upkeep of the floats and carts, costumes, and attendant expenses. All ages are recruited, from the young boys who sit atop the floats playing instruments, to the men who slowly pull the massively heavy floats through the streets. Another two men stand astride the front of each float giving directions with a delft flicks of handheld fans. Despite the sweltering heat and hours of organizing, participation in this cultural heritage is a coveted honor.

The floats themselves have been transformed into moving museums with heavy European tapestries and ornate lengths of Chinese embroidered silk that traders brought into the county over 400 years ago. To the Japa-

nese artisans and merchants with the prescience to recognize the novel beauty of these imported fabrics, the subtly colored pigments and elegantly fine needlework bespoke different cultures and societies; they conjured worlds inhabited by unknown artists whose skills were revealed through their handiwork.

The Aoi Festival on May 15 is a procession and pageant that takes a whole day to unfold. Glistening black oxen pull black lacquered carriages dripping with wisteria blossoms through the streets of Kyoto. Ladies in ancient court attire sit resplendent inside. Attendants and men dressed as courtiers walk alongside. They all accompany the female messenger of the Imperial court as she bears a greeting to the chief priest of the Kamigamo Shrine. Along the way, the procession stops at the Shimogamo Shrine where "courtiers" in ancient garb display archery

skills. They shoot their arrows while perched on wooden saddles set on bedecked and tasseled horses. After a break for refreshment in the shrine, the procession continues through the streets and along the Kamo River. The hypnotically slow pace and the creaky swaying motion of the ox-drawn carts impart an atmosphere of timelessness.

Kyoto's third great festival, Jidai Matsuri is held annually on October 22. This newer Festival of the Ages showcases Kyoto's 1,200-year history in a visual display of the city's position as arbiter of design and tradition. Costumes reflect back a thousand years to when women of the 9th century court donned twelve layers of diaphanous silk *kimono*. The display extends into the late 19th century, when the appearance of Japanese men in suit and tie signaled the country's opening to Western fashion, culture, and science.

Even today, the weaving and dyeing industries of Kyoto continue to contribute their artistic acumen in researching and renewing the intricate weaves and dyes that reflects centuries of textile techniques.

In addition to providing a gorgeous entertainment for native and tourist alike, Kyoto's festive pageantry continues after a thousand years to reassure believers that the gods remain aware of their petitioners' desire for safety and peace.

Above left Dancing flames and flying sparks electrify the evening sky as Mountain Ascetic monks (Yamabushi) of the Shingon Buddhist sect prepare the coals for the annual fire-walking ceremony in which participants pray for prolonged good health. The summer event is held at Tanukidani Fudomyo-in temple located up an approach steep enough to ably test one's health and endurance.

Bottom right (clockwise from top left) A young man in formal festival wear on the morning of a procession. The designs on the clothing identifies to which float the participant is connected.

One event during the Gion Festival is the Flowered Hat procession (Hanagasa) during which the sacred oracle, symbolically personified as a young boy (*chigo*), is mounted on horseback and led through the streets. His two young attendants are also mounted, accompanied by their *kimono*-clad mothers.

The *biwa* is a lute that reached Japan centuries ago via the Silk Road, and became part of Japan's musical heritage. The five-stringed lute's dulcet tones provide accompaniment for famous ballads as well as being played as a solo instrument.

A banner is carried beside the warrior-clad boy in the morning procession as part of the Yasaka Shrine festival. The helmet indicates the family's clan.

Above middle Japan's largest and most popular shrine is Fushimi Inari Taisha, founded in 711, in the southeastern district of Kyoto. On a summer evening of July 21, red lanterns illuminate the shrine precincts during the Motomiya Festival as visitors walk through hundreds of red *torii* gates to pray for prosperity. The view is of the Roumon Gate.

Above right The month of July is filled with events connected to the Gion Matsuri festival, including processions of massive floats on July 17 and 24 bringing Kyoto's treasures into public view. *Yukata*-clad men at the bow of the Ofune Hoko, are pulling the boat-shaped float with twisted straw ropes through the streets. Young boys similarly clad sit on the upper level of the boat performing *Gion-bayashi* music on flutes and cymbals.

GARDENS OF KYOTO

The gardens of Kyoto incorporate the history of the city in a horticultural heritage that is unique in the world. The flora of the archipelago provides a rich array of color and scent that were blended with romantic yearnings, poetic literature, and ritual settings to provide a daily backdrop for a society that loves gardens so much it brought them inside. A distinctively shaped rock expertly placed in a dwelling's inner garden allows the family god to descend graciously into the residence; a lovingly trimmed and cared for pine planted in the compound brings spiritual security throughout generations; a humble night-blooming cereus provides a shared occasion to watch petals languidly unfold and release their scent into dark summer air; on a full-moon autumn night, a potted tuff of pampas on a narrow porch invites people to enjoy the grass's fluttering shadows on a paper door.

A thousand years ago, families in the capital with large estates created personal landscapes. Within walled compounds, nobles strolled along the narrow paths around the house, or perhaps boarded a shallow-bottomed boat to refresh the view with a shoreline perspective. Raised on pillars, their one-storied buildings seemed not bound to earth, but rather

gave the impression of a winged creature that had serendipitously alighted on ground.

The ancient gardens of the nobility were spacious and grand. But eventually, population increases, more complex social structures, and destruction by warring factions mandated more compact grounds.

Religion also played a part in landscaping. In the 14th century, Muso Kokushi designed the famed moss garden in Arashiyama that introduced a meditative tenant that became the signature of Zen sub-temple complexes. The sect's teachings of self-discipline and a spare lifestyle were reflected in minimalist gardens, where the concentration of space focused the eye on specific spiritual concepts. Frugally raked sand, for example, swirling around mounds of moss, or a fern nestled against a rock introduced an abstract symbol that many regard as the most distinguishing feature of all Japanese garden design.

Zen temples, also centers of learning and spiritual pursuit, became reserves of the arts of calligraphy and tea ceremony, which emerged as forms of discipline and entertainment. Minimalist conceits were at the heart of teahouse design, which eschewed, for example, flowers that might distract by

their color or fragrance. Entering a tearoom meant leaving behind the secular world for a more spiritually aesthetic realm.

Many private spaces—once statements of power and elitism available only to warlords and their followers—are now botanical gardens and parks open to "commoners." Visitors can seek solace in the lushness of curving paths, leafy shade, and murmuring iris-lined streams.

Wandering the streets of the ancient capital today visitors to

Kyoto can enjoy not only magnificent landscapes but the joys of tiny, gem-like gardens. Some feature decades-old potted plants. Some host horticultural wonders such as flamboyant azalea or serene pine bonsai, or the meter-high chrysanthemums that take a full year of the gardener's time to bring to maturity. No matter how small the dwelling, the floral traditions and numerous temple gardens of Kyoto are testament to the Japanese delight and respect for nature.

Top left The message in a Zen temple often resides in its visual detail. The simplicity of the circular raked sand framing a stone alludes to a spiritual concept.

Top middle A woman standing on the arched stone bridge spanning the lotus pond in the Zen temple of Nanzen-ji reflects upon the meaning of the lotus in which one emerges from the mud and ascends to a pure state of heart and mind.

Top right Kyoto lays in a semi-tropical zone which makes it necessary to wrap some of its greenery in braided straw to protect against winter's frosty bite.

Above left The red carpet is laid out to invite visitors to sit and enjoy a bowl of powdered green tea if they wish. Seated on the floor, one can enjoy the view from Hosen-in temple in the village of Ohara.

Above Once considered outside the capital, the Jodo-sect temple of Honen-in is nestled against the eastern hills. The thatched gate indicates its rustic nature and centuries-old isolation from the capital.

Left Once the private residence of renowned landscape designer, Mirei Shigemori, the house is located on the west side of Yoshida Shrine. Occasionally open to visitors, Shigemori's eclectic use of large stones empowers the space with energy and vitality.

Above A visitor pauses to admire the early autumn hues emerging in the stroll garden in the south part of Tenju-an, a sub temple of Nanzen-ji.

CHAPTER 2

CENTRAL AND EASTERN KYOTO

HERITAGE SIGHTS OF CENTRAL AND EASTERN KYOTO

Kyoto's central district features many of the easiest to access and best-known sights in the ancient capital. The former Imperial Palace and its surrounding park, marked by the large green rectangular area in the center of all Kyoto maps, is open 24 hours a day. The palace site features tiny shrines, two ponds, a meandering stream and the official State Guest House, as well as traces of the former estates of courtiers and aristocrats.

Kyoto's beloved Kiyomizu, a World Heritage Site, sits atop one of the 36 peaks that form the Eastern Mountains.

The central streets are easy to navigate and those in the foothills slope gently upwards. The pace is slow and leisurely, perfect for a day of visiting the former palace, temples, shrines and shops that tempt the eye along the way.

Above The pagoda on the Eastern Hills of the Kiyomizu Temple complex against the evening sky.

Above Two clay foxes, symbols of fecundity, guard a small Shinto shrine.

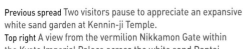

Previous spread Two visitors pause to appreciate an expansive white sand garden at Kennin-ji Temple.
Top right A view from the vermilion Nikkamon Gate within the Kyoto Imperial Palace across the white sand Dantei inner garden courtyard of the Shishinden Ceremonial Hall to Gekkamon Gate.
Left During the Shichigosan Festival in October, parents take their three- and seven-year-old daughters, such as these two girls, and five-year-old sons to shrines to pray for their child's growth and good health
Right The Kamo River banks are wide and well landscaped, giving Kyoto inhabitants a chance to escape the confines of the ancient city, stretch their legs and admire views of the mountains that border the city.

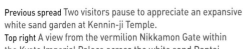

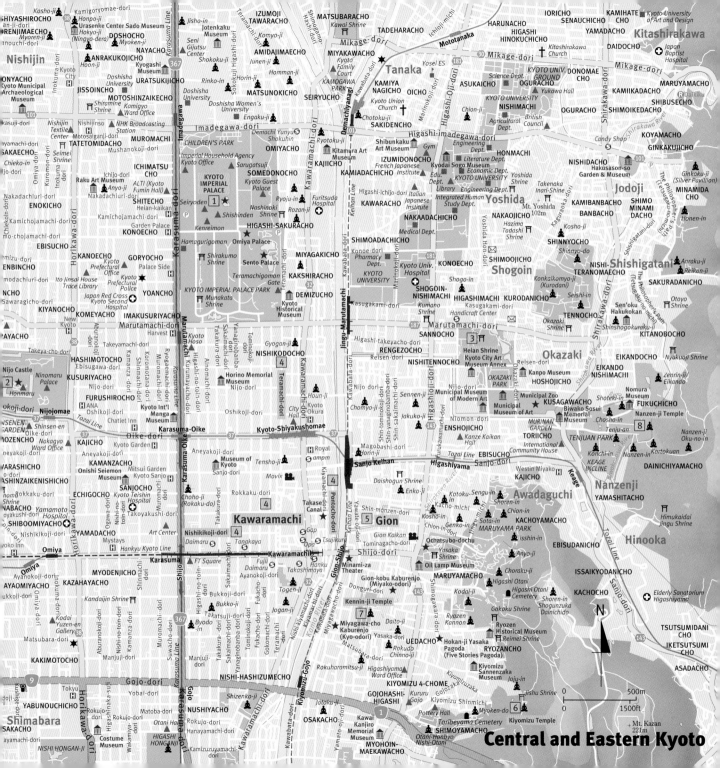

Central and Eastern Kyoto

KYOTO'S IMPERIAL PALACE

Visitors can easily slip back 150 years in the Imperial Park that surrounds the former Imperial Palace. Until the Emperor moved to Tokyo in 1868, the spacious grounds were home to more than 100 aristocrats. Today, their names are inscribed on markers scattered among the large boulders and stately old trees, the remains of their private estates and gardens.

Today, much of the parkland is public: student sports groups jog outside the wall of the inner palace, parents mind barefooted toddlers wading in the narrow stream in the southwest side, dog walkers meet and chat along the large gravel-covered paths. There are tennis courts, baseball mounds and a small court for gate-ball, a croquet-like sport popular with older people.

The two former Imperial residences, Kyoto Gosho in the center of the park and Sento Gosho in the southeast corner, require permission to enter, obtained from the Imperial Household Agency in the northwest corner.

The entrance gates to the inner palace are formidable structures, magnificent in their own right. The largest, Kenreimon, faces directly south and was accessible solely by the Emperor. The east gate, Kenshumon, was for the Empress. The architecture exemplifies the restrained beauty that is so characteristic of Japanese art and is a marvel of ancient carpentry traditions.

Twice a year, in the spring and fall, the inner palace is open to the public. The Shishin-den, or main building (destroyed by fire and rebuilt in 1855), is where new emperors are enthroned. Its gates are brilliant vermilion, but the inner palace buildings are of unpainted wood with huge, curved cypress bark roofs.

The smaller hall, the Shunko-den, contains the sacred mirror of the Imperial family, a symbol of Imperial presence used only on special occasions. It harkens back to ancient mythology when the sun goddess, Amaterasu-no-Omi-kami, emerged from a cave, bringing light back into the world. Shrine mirrors, often of bronze, reflect the light of the sun as it passes along the southern horizon, and remain one of the essential possessions of Shinto shrines.

The front courtyard of Shishin-den is of the purest white gravel. Japanese believe that in such sacred spaces, known as *yuniwa*, one can sense the presence of deities and it is here that they listen to the petitions of their devotees.

Entrance to the interior rooms is not permitted, but its gardens are compact masterpieces of landscaping and worth seeing.

The outer Imperial Park is also well maintained by the same special corps of specially trained gardeners. The plum, peach and cherry trees are among the most popular destinations in spring, and the park's ponds and old-growth trees a haven for birds.

Opposite Open twice a year to the general public and upon request, the brilliant cinnabar-colored doors of the former Imperial Palace reveal an expansive inner courtyard.

Below The outer walls of the palace are constructed of stone and clay, the five white lines denoting an Imperial dwelling. Massive gates, cypress bark roofs and slate gray funneled roof tiles belie Japan's preference for understated design in carpentry and masonry skills.

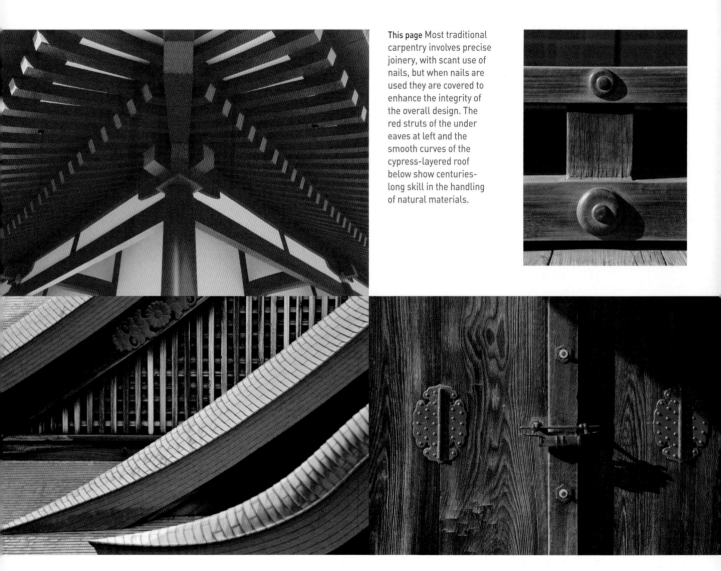

This page Most traditional carpentry involves precise joinery, with scant use of nails, but when nails are used they are covered to enhance the integrity of the overall design. The red struts of the under eaves at left and the smooth curves of the cypress-layered roof below show centuries-long skill in the handling of natural materials.

Left Frolicking tigers depicted on the sliding doors of the Tiger Room in Shodaibunoma Hall at Kyoto Imperial Palace. Above Paintings of two Chinese immortals enhance wooden sliding doors.

Right Tranquil and sedate, the panoramic backdrop of the Eastern Hills highlights the elegant lines of an arched stone bridge in the grounds of Sento Imperial Palace.

NIJO
CASTLE

Like its European counterpart, this castle, the administrative center for the Tokugawa Shogunate who ruled Japan from 1615 to 1868, has a moat. But there the similarities end. While Nijo's gate is imposing and its earthen walls thick, it is the ornate rooms, gold foil-backed screens and exotic stroll garden that wielded the power to intimidate enemies.

At Ninomaru Palace is a gold-highlighted, elaborately carved wooden Chinese Gate brought from a warlord's castle in Fushimi. The carriage entrance is precursor to the *genkan*, where guests, even today, shed their outer clothing and remove their footwear.

The palace rooms lie in diagonal succession. Guests entered only as far as rank allowed, with a select few permitted into the farthest chamber where the Shogun conducted business.

More practical than aesthetic, the garden beside the main room is an expanse of rocks (gifts from different provinces) and short, stout cycad palms that offer no place to hide. The inner *uguisu-bari*, or nightingale floors, also designed for defense, "chirp" when trod on to alert guards to an intruder.

The art in the inner audience rooms, painted by Kano Tanyu (1602–74), embodies wealth and strength, with hawks, tigers and huge powerful creatures rampant on gold leaf surfaces. Ohiroma, the most impressive room, where the Shogun met the highest officials, is painted with images of magnificent pines. Rather than a display of weaponry, a room large enough to accommodate this artwork illustrated the ruler's power.

The ponds, exotic trees and paths through the outer gardens are as much a reminder of the residential environment of Japan's military class as the buildings themselves. The gardens are especially lovely in the cherry blossom season and are lit nightly.

Above The gates of the outer wall at Nijo Castle, a World Heritage Site, are open to visitors.
Left A family visits the castle's garden in spring.

Above Originating along China's Silk Road, elaborate fretwork remains an integral part of Japan's design tradition.
Above left Traffic streams by the southeast corner of the spotlit castle turret.

From left to right Granite steps lead to the western entrance of the castle complex. Gold was employed to lighten the interior and denote the wealth of the resident warlord. Stepping stones were sent as gifts to the warlord from farflung prefectures. Gardeners are needed all year round to maintain the castle's extensive grounds.

NIJO CASTLE

HEIAN JINGU
THE SHRINE OF PEACE AND TRANQUILITY

The magnificent *torii* gate on Jingu-michi Street, south of the main entrance to Heian Shrine, marks the shrine as a major tourist attraction, and justifiably so. Curiously, given the hundreds of shrines in the city, this is one of the newest.

Heian Jingu was constructed in 1895 to commemorate 1,100 years of the city's founding, and dedicated to emperors Kammu (Kyoto's first emperor, 794) and Komei (1831–67, father of the Meiji Emperor).

The setting is a little east of the Kamo River, thus outside the ancient city proper, but a splendid site to construct one of the city's most gorgeous stroll gardens.

The present buildings, with their vermilion woodwork and green tile roofs, closely resemble the original palace but were constructed at two-thirds the original size. Ablaze in sunlight, they are a notable testament to Japanese carpentry skills. Entrance to the shrine is free, but the expansive stroll garden requires a fee.

Designed by Ogawa Jihei (1860–1933), one of Kyoto's foremost gardeners, the grounds blend contemporary and ancient aesthetics. Copious and innovative use of flowering plants is incorporated into the millennium-old layout favored by Heian nobles.

Paths first wind through the hanging cherry garden, an incomparable display of deep pink blossoms in April, possibly one of the loveliest places on earth when in bloom. The first pond, surrounded by azalea bushes and long-stemmed irises, is best seen in May and June. The stepping stones in the pond were formed from the stone pillars from Gojo and Sanjo bridge supports. The pond beyond has a variety of later blooming azaleas and water lilies in June. The unadorned wooden bridge that crosses the pond was moved here from a former Imperial palace and has bench seating that allows visitors a restful view of the grounds.

In early June, when the open courtyard is the setting for torch-lit Noh plays during the evenings, the shrine provides an exotic backdrop to this traditional form of drama.

This is a popular shrine for parents to come and ask the Shinto gods for blessings for their three-, five- and seven-year old children and for weddings in the special hall to the east of the Main Hall. The gods play a vital part in dispensing their grace on newborns, the growth of children and young couples, so many supplicants come especially on those occasions.

Opposite Proud parents snap a photo of their formally dressed daughter in the late afternoon sun.
Above The view from the bridge that spans the cherry-lined pond at Heian Shrine, a structure that once was part of a former Imperial palace.
Right The "tail of the dragon" stepping stones caution visitors to mind their step when crossing the pond.

Above The main exhibition hall of Heian Shrine contains shards of ancient tiles that belonged to the estate of an emperor's consort. A replica of a former Imperial palace, the shrine presents a page of architectural history with its Chinese-influenced symmetry.
Right Peering through the closed door, a visitor awaits entry.
Far right Women visitors enjoy the tranquil view of the garden's pond.

| CENTRAL AND EASTERN KYOTO

Left *Picture Scroll of Annual Rites and Ceremonies*, a 12th century source of ancient buildings in the capital, has been used in hip-and-gable construction. The addition of roof tiles began in the 6th century as Chinese building techniques began to enter Japan. Both building traditions merge within the capital's buildings. **Above** The soft rustle of silk marks the passing of a shrine maiden.

DOWNTOWN
KYOTO

KAWARAMACHI, NISHIKI, TERAMACHI AND PONTOCHO

Central Kyoto's streets and alleys teem with shoppers, business people, tourists, students and sightseers. They are drawn by the department stores, boutiques, restaurants, banks and food markets that line Kawaramachi and Teramachi, between Sanjo and Shijo-dori, and Nishiki-koji, from Teramachi to Karasuma.

Kyoto's downtown district has not changed much in centuries. Now, cars and modern dress replace carts and traditional dress and glitzy neon and colorful lettering supplant the subdued hand-carved signs once mounted

Above Seated at the busy downtown section of Sanjo and Kawabata-dori is an image of a top-knotted *samurai*, Takayama Hikokuro (1747–93), who shows his respect to the Emperor by bowing in the direction of the Imperial Palace.

over shop entrances, but the entrepreneurial spirit remains.

Some streets, such as Kawaramachi-dori, did not exist 1,000 years ago. The easternmost street then was Kyogoku (now called Shinkyogoku or New Kyogoku Street) that runs parallel to Kawaramachi on the west.

To the east, Kawaramachi was bordered by the Kamo River, an overflowing torrent during heavy rain but reduced to a shallow flowing stream within a vast sandy expanse. Realizing that when the river was low the city was vulnerable to attack, the war-

lord Hideyoshi (1536–98) began a project to reshape the capital by enclosing it with a large earthen wall and building sturdy bridges. Sanjo Bridge, constructed in 1590, still closely resembles depictions of the original bridge seen in old woodblock prints.

The Kamo River banks were home to entertainers, precursors of Kabuki, while the narrow nearby Takase River carried charcoal and cords of wood to the pottery kilns along Gojo Street in the central eastern part of the city.

Over the centuries, the defensive earthen walls that confined

and guarded the city's eastern flank disintegrated and Kyoto pushed east. Eventually, the expanded area to the east of the Kamo River became home to the villas and ateliers of wealthier citizens and artists.

Teramachi (literally, Temple District) got its name when Hideyoshi moved many temples to this street and to Shinkyogoku. His goal was not to show off Kyoto's religious heritage to travelers, but to provide defense if the city were attacked from the east.

Today, some shops still sell religious goods: altar ornaments,

Top left Two women ascend the multi-storied escalator at Kyoto Station.
Above left Mendicant monks with alms bowl extended appear occasionally on Shijo and Sanjo bridges.
Above The narrow street that runs through Pontocho, one of Kyoto's main *geiko* districts, is lined with some of the city's most traditional architecture. The bordering *ochaya* (teahouses) are lit with lanterns welcoming guests and the *maiko* and *geiko* who will provide entertainment for the evening.

Left In full bloom, April's cherry trees extend their blossoms over the canal-like Takase River.
Below left Giant chopsticks mounted over the entrance of this "chopsticks gallery." No Japanese traveler can resist buying souvenirs, and Teramachi and Shinkyogoku streets are the places to go.
Below right Lanterns with the names of patrons and shop names all contribute to Nishiki Tenmangu Shrine so that the gods may continue to favor them.
Bottom left This young boy's clothing marks his participation in one of the city's many festivals.
Right Nishiki-koji is *the* main shopping market street, selling all the delicacies that please the Japanese palette.

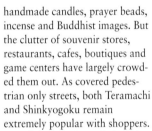

handmade candles, prayer beads, incense and Buddhist images. But the clutter of souvenir stores, restaurants, cafes, boutiques and game centers have largely crowded them out. As covered pedestrian only streets, both Teramachi and Shinkyogoku remain extremely popular with shoppers.

Nishiki-koji (Brocade Street) does not reflect its name. Originally called Gusoku-koji, this wide street was where warriors' armor was forged and sold. But the name, pronounced quickly, sounds unhappily like Excrement Street. The dismayed Emperor renamed it "brocade" in 1054 to complement Twill Street (Aya no Koji) two blocks south, thereby protecting Kyoto's reputation as a refined aristocratic capital.

About 300 years ago, as the demand for armor decreased, the convenient location drew fishmongers and other food vendors. Many items are displayed along the arcade, uncovered and within inches of onlookers, so that strolling along the narrow street is a visual and olfactory adventure, even for locals. Prices are higher than at local supermarkets, but customers, from housewives to discerning chefs from Kyoto's finest restaurants, rely on the quality of the vendors, whose reputations can go back generations.

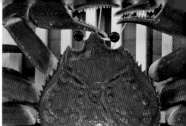

From top to bottom Words are not needed to find this restaurant with its large mounted animatronic crustacean at the corner of Sanjo and Teramachi streets. Crab, mostly from the chilly depths of the Japan Sea, is its specialty. A downtown resident cycling with her young son seated up front. Waiting for a friend? Many restaurants line the Kamo River. This one, aglow with convivial customers, is beside the Shijo Bridge.

THE GION DISTRICT

The traditional entertainment districts of Gion, Pontocho, Shimabara, Miyagawa-cho and Kamishichiken have especially beautiful restaurants and *ochaya* (establishments which offer *geiko* and *maiko* performances). The refined gait of a *maiko*, gorgeously attired in *kimono* with lacquered paper umbrella in hand, passing the dark-fronted houses, presents an exotic opportunity to appreciate a moment of grace. The refined bow of a *geiko* as she enters a place of entertainment, a glimpse of a flowing silken sleeve as the door slides quietly shut, bring another dimension to beauty in these districts.

In Kyoto, *geisha* are known as *geiko*, the term meaning a woman accomplished in the arts. Her understudy is a *maiko*, a young woman who apprentices, usually from age sixteen, at the *okiya* in the *geiko* districts of Gion, Pontocho, Miyagawa-cho and Kamishichiken.

Left Flowing down from Mount Hiei, the narrow, picturesque Shirakawa River passes through Gion and offers refuge to migrating ducks and a home to tricolored carp.

The Western sexualization of this ancient practice is both unfortunate and inaccurate. The *gei* in *geiko* refers to the arts, usually the performing arts of singing, dancing and playing musical instruments, including the *shamisen*, a three-stringed banjo-like instrument. The *mai* in *maiko* means dance, one of the first skills a young woman learns, because moving gracefully in a *kimono* requires practice, good posture and elegant, controlled bearing.

But to see *kimono* at their most magnificent, the beautiful streets that traverse Gion and Pontocho districts and their adjacent theaters are the places to go. There, you can step back hundreds of years to glimpse a *maiko* passing the elegant old wooden teahouses on her way to her music lesson or hairdresser. It is almost like spotting a rare bird, and as the *maiko* comes into view, throngs of camera-wielding tourists congregate, seemingly emerging from nowhere, to capture the excitement of the moment. On occasion, so many people gather that volunteer guides must keep them from impeding the *maiko's* elegant passage.

The buildings lining the streets of Pontocho and Gion are another of Kyoto's treasures. The soft-colored wooden lattice doors that slide soundlessly open to reveal miniature gardens and stone paths are as beautiful as they are distinctive. The *ochaya* teahouse differs from the dwellings of ordinary residents. The buildings are constructed of many small

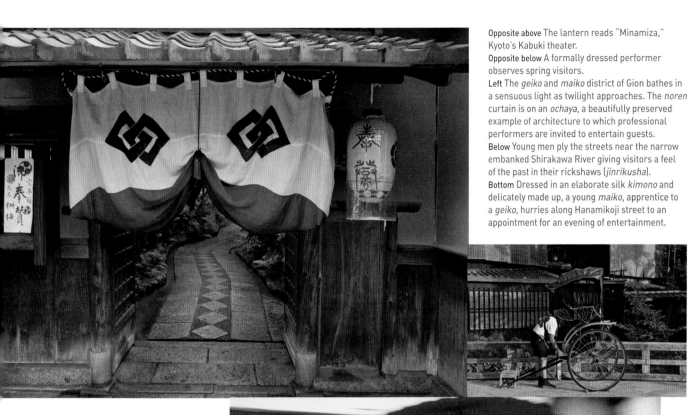

rooms, some with alcoves displaying a treasured object and flower arrangement. Within these rooms, guests assemble. The crystal clear flow of *sake* as it is poured into tiny delicate cups and the many courses are accompanied by the swish of a silk *kimono* and the graceful demeanor of the server. The seemingly effortless elegance by which a dinner proceeds defines an evening well spent and encompasses the essence of the *geisha* districts.

KIYOMIZU-DERA
THE TEMPLE OF
PURE WATER

Named after the pure healing waters that flow from Otowa no Taki waterfall, the World Heritage Site of Kiyomizu is older than the city, founded by General Sakanoue no Tamuramaro and given to the priest Enchin in 780.

For over 1,000 years, suppliants, some on their knees, ascended the two main staired streets known as the "two-year slope" and the "three-year slope" to offer prayers to the Goddess of Mercy. The street names came from a superstition that if one tumbled on the age-softened stones, that person would incur two or three years of misfortune.

On both sides of the entrance to the complex is the gate with muscular Nio temple guardians, both challenging the evil beliefs of those attempting to pass between them. The gate (1478) is one of the oldest structures in the complex (the Sutra Hall is oldest).

The Main Hall, rebuilt in 1633, is a magnificent structure with an extended "dancing platform" supported by massive beams that form the scaffolding beneath, a 400-year-old marvel of engineered joinery without nails. In the cool, dark recesses behind the main altar, gilded bodhisattvas glimmer dimly, adding to the mystical atmosphere. The main figure, Kannon, the Bodhisattva of Mercy, is so sacred that it is only displayed every 30 years, with the next opportunity in 2024.

Top A child ladles water from the spout of the "Sound of Feathers Waterfall."
Above Some of the renowned blossoms of Kiyomizu.

Top right Brilliant cinnabar-colored struts of the Ro-mon Tower Gate.
Above right Stylized impression of Buddha's footprints are carved in stone.

The path to Okuno-in, another building supported by scaffolding, offers a spectacular view of the Main Hall and the city beyond. In the late afternoon, the sun bathes the halls in a rosy glow, peeling away centuries and evoking the time when pilgrims traveled far to see this magical vista that remains one of Kyoto's most popular tourist destinations.

The waterfall flowing from the mountain, from which the temple takes its name, has been divided into three channels, with long-handled dippers available for visitors to sample its efficacious water.

Walking farther along the wooded pathway leads to the three-tiered pagoda and another panoramic view of the Main Hall and Okuno-in, the second pavilion.

The Higashiyama (Eastern Mountains) district around the temple is rich in color and craft. Rickshaws swoop around the hilly terrain carrying tourists. Tiny twisting streets and alleyways are lined with shops selling *shichimi-togarashi*, seasoned chili powder, while characteristic arch-shaped baked sweets, *yatsuhashi*, permeate the air with the aroma of cinnamon.

Thrilled and embarrassed by the attention they draw, young women visitors, professionally dressed in the gorgeous *kimono* and *obi* worn by *maiko*, stroll the streets, snapping each other's photos and posing for tourists.

Antique shops, cafes and eateries catering to all tastes fill the Higashiyama area, and shops still feature the characteristic porcelain ceramics and enameled stoneware. Generations of potters took advantage of the foothill's updraft to evenly fire their pottery in climbing kilns on the slopes until pollution laws in the 1950s required them to relocate.

Higashiyama offers many pleasures, from window shopping to visiting a temple that predates Kyoto, while the area's playful and relaxed atmosphere encourages one to linger for hours.

KENNIN-JI
TEMPLE

Enter the Kennin-ji complex in its busy midtown setting and the city fades away.

The monk Eisai (1141–1241) founded this Rinzai temple in 1202, making it the oldest of Kyoto's Zen temples. The Rinzai sect emphasizes reaching enlightenment through sudden understanding, aided by pondering a *koan*. By giving the student this conundrum with no rational answer, the teacher spurs the acolyte to higher awareness.

Kennin-ji, like the other Zen temples in Kyoto, is laid out in Chinese style in a grid pattern based on a north–south axis, with subtemples and small gardens constructed in Japanese style lining the periphery. An immense hall in the center of the compound houses an image of Shakamuni flanked by two attendant images.

Recent renovations allow visi-

tors to enter the Abbot's Quarters and the buildings connected to it via tiled roof corridors. The doors have been removed to allow views of the expansive *kare-sansui* sand and rock garden. Zen gardens are for contemplation, an aid in transcending the mundane through the abstract principles implied in the rocks and sand. One popular interpretation of this garden is the grouping of three standing rocks in the raked sand, often thought of as representing Buddha and two acolytes. The sumptuously green moss garden is called the Sound of the Tide Garden. With its soft undulating mounds of star moss, it is as soothing to the eyes as the former is stimulating, evoking entirely different images and reflections.

In 2002, Kennin-ji celebrated its 800th anniversary and commissioned artist Koizumi Junsaku (1924–2012) to paint two majestic twin dragons charging through the heavens, the wish-granting jewel in one five-taloned claw. The ink painting, on thick Japanese paper, was attached to

Opposite Soft mounds of moss in the Main Hall's garden offer visitors an opportunity to sit and ponder life.
Left A bowl of whisked green tea and a sweet for someone.
Below A dry landscape garden (*kare-sansui*) beyond the cusped window
Bottom left The art of combining gravel, stone and sand.
Bottom center A young visitor rests in a priest's chair.
Bottom right Perfect raked arcs of sand at the end of a wooden plank veranda.

the ceiling of Nenge-do Hall.

Other halls open to the public contain sliding *fusuma* doors painted by famous Kyoto artists, and include Hashimoto Kansetsu's depiction of the Zen principles in "The Cycle of Death and Rebirth." The temple gallery features replicas of painted screens (the originals are in the Kyoto National Museum) of the thunder gods, Fujin and Raijin.

A few steps away from Kyoto's busiest intersection, Kennin-ji, an active monastery, remains a world apart from its secular neighbors.

NANZEN-JI
TEMPLE

Resting at the wooded foothills of the Eastern Mountains, Nanzen-ji, was once the villa of the retired emperor Kameyama, and was converted into a Rinzai Zen temple in 1291.

The Sanmon Gate and most of the structures date to the early 17th century. Shoes in hand, a very steep climb and a narrow bridge lead to the second floor. Although the wall paintings and views are lovely, the real attraction is historic. Ishikawa Goemon, a well-known thief, a Japanese version of Robin Hood, was captured there and sentenced to death in 1594 by boiling in a cauldron. In times past, many houses had fire-heated cast iron tubs in their bathrooms, which became known as Goemon-buro, and thus giving the thief a place in bathing nomenclature.

The Hojo (Abbot's Quarters) contains famous paintings by the Kano School masters and an expansive garden of raked white gravel, enclosed by an earthen wall, itself an object of beauty.

The subtemples all have beautifully crafted grounds and art-work, and Tenju-an's north garden as well as its south-facing stroll garden and carp pond were recently re-landscaped.

The resplendent carved gate of black lacquer in Konchi-an dates from 1628, and serves as a shrine to the Tokugawa Shogun who bestowed the temple to its first abbot. Konchi-in's classic Zen garden evokes the shapes of a crane and a tortoise, symbolizing longevity and immortality.

A unique and remarkably beautiful structure on the east side of the grounds is an arched brick conduit carrying water into the city from Lake Biwa. After the Meiji Emperor moved to Edo (now Tokyo), the city of Kyoto feared it would suffer from a loss of its well-established influential classes and undertook several noteworthy projects. This was one. Tunnels had to be blasted through the Eastern Mountains, bricks fired and carried here to start construction on the country's first hydroelectric water plant. This symbol of 120-year-old technology blends seamlessly with the existing Buddhist antiquity,

Opposite *Ishi-tatami*, a term which means the placement of stones as found in *tatami* rooms. The granite and moss approach to the temple is a masterpiece of simplicity.
Above A view of visitors from the massive gate.
Right The long veranda of Seiryoden Hall is constructed so that support columns do not obstruct the view of the Hojo Zen garden.
Below A shoreline of moss and rock at the edge of raked sand.

Below left Gigantic round posts support the Main Gate of the complex.
Below right Young visitors conferring where to go next.

a reminder of the city's pride in its religious traditions and innovative skills.

The Nanzen-ji complex is especially crowded in autumn, when the canopy of stately deep green pines allows the lower maple trees to set the grounds ablaze with color.

Below Shaping this pine tree took years of study and a whole day to trim.
Right Elegant in its ancient shape, the final stages of beauty are appreciated in aged trees.

Above Early morning sun warms two visitors under the Main Gate.
Top right Whisked tea and a sweet await the visitor.
Center right Fine patterns of moss, stone and raked gravel in the side garden at Tenju-an.
Right *Oni-gawara* are the demon-faced tiles set at ends of a main roof ridge to deflect evil spirits from approaching a sacred place.

CHAPTER 3
NORTHERN KYOTO

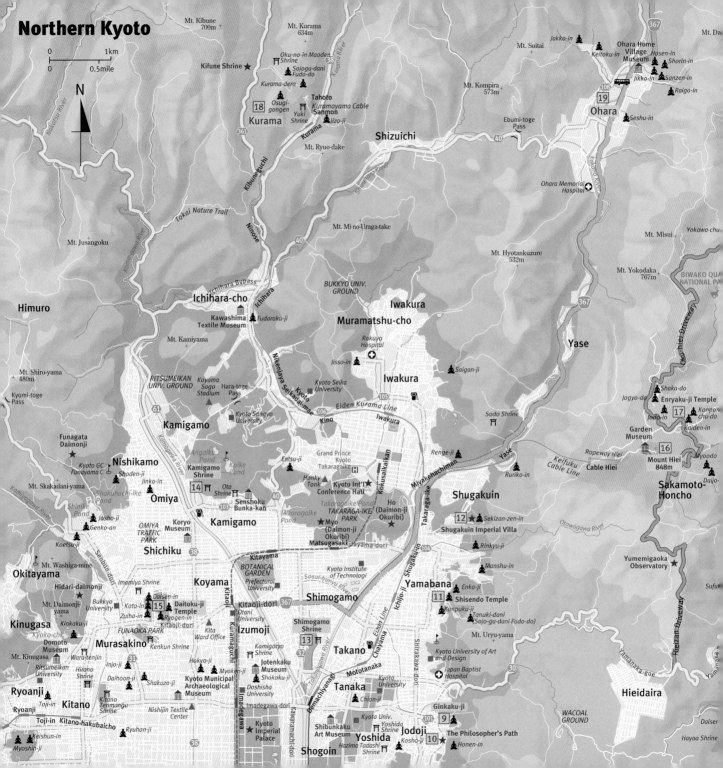

Northern Kyoto

0   1km
0   0.5mile

N

Mt. Kibune 700m
Mt. Kurama 634m
Mt. Suitai
Mt. Da
Jakko-in
Keitoku-in
Ohara Home Village Museum
Hosen-in
Shorin-in
Kifune Shrine ★
Oku-no-in Maoden
Sojoga-dani Fudo-do
Jikko-in
Sanzen-in
Kurama-dera
Raigo-in
Osugi-gongen
Tahoto
Kuramayama Cable Sanmon
19
18
Yuki Shrine
Jizo-ji
Ohara
Seshu-in
Kurama
Kurama
Mt. Kompira 573m
361
Mt. Ryuo-dake
Shizuichi
Ebumi-toge Pass
40
Mt. Mi-no-Uraga-take
Mt. Misui
Yokawa-chu
Kibuneguchi
Tokai Nature Trail
Ninose
Ohara Memorial Hospital
Mt. Jusangoku
Mt. Hyotankuzure 532m
Mt. Yokodaka 767m
BIWAKO QUA
NATIONAL PA
Ichihara Bypass
BUKKYO UNIV. GROUND
Ichihara-cho
Iwakura
Yase
Ichihara
Muramatsu-cho
Himuro
Kawashima Textile Museum
Fudaraku-ji
Rakuyo Hospital
Mt. Kamiyama
Jisso-ji
Iwakura
Saigan-ji
RITSUMEIKAN UNIV. GROUND
Koyama Sogo Stadium
Hara-toge Pass
Kyoto Seika University
Shaka-do
Mt. Shiro-yama 480m
Jogyo-do
Enryaku-ji Temple
Kyomi-toge Pass
61
Kyoto Sangyo University
Eiden Kurama Line
106
17
Konpon-chu-o
Jodo-in
Kamigamo
Kino
Iwakura
Sodo Shrine
Kaidan-in
Funagata Daimonji
Kyoto GC Funayama C
Shoden-ji
Nishikamo
Jinko-in
Renge-ji
Ruriko-in
Yase
Garden Museum
16
Mount Hiei 848m
Myoodo
Mt. Skakadani-yama
Josho-ji
Arigaike Pond
Kamigamo Shrine
Entsu-ji
Grand Prince Kyoto Takaragaike
Keifuku Cable Line
Cable Hiei
Sakamoto-Honcho
Shinike Pond
14
Ota Shrine
Honky Tonk
Kokusaikaikan
Miyakehachiman
Shakuhachi-ike Pond
Omiya
Senshoku Bunka-kan
Kyoto Int'l Conference Hall
Shugakuin
Genko-an
103
Ho (Daimon-ji Okuribi)
Takaraga-ike
Koetsu-ji
Kamigamo
40
Mizorogaike Pond
TAKARAGA-IKE PARK
12
Sekizan-zen-in
OMIYA TRAFFIC PARK
Koryo Museum
Myo (Daimon-ji Okuribi)
Shugakuin Imperial Villa
Otowagawa River
Mt. Washiga-mine
Shichiku
38
Matsugasaki
Kitayama-dori
Rinkyu-ji
Yumemigaoka Observatory
Okitayama
Hidari-daimonji
Kitayama
BOTANICAL GARDEN
Kyoto Institute of Technologi
Manshu-in
Imamiya Shrine
Koyama
Prefectural University
Sosui-bunui Line
Yamabana
Bukkyo University
Koto-in
Daisen-in
Daitoku-ji Temple
Shimogamo
Enko-ji
11
Shisendo Temple
Mt. Daimonji-yama
15
Zuiho-in
Ryogen-in
Kitaoji-dori
Konpuku-in
Tanuki-dani (Sojo-ga-dani Fudo-do)
Kinugasa
Kinkaku-ji
Otani University
Kita Ward Office
Izumoji
367
Shimogamo Shrine
Mt. Uryu-yama
Mt. Kinugasa
Domoto Museum
FUNAOKA PARK
Kuramaguchi
13
Kyoto University of Art and Design
Ritsumeikan University
Wara-tenjin
Murasakino
Kenkun Shrine
32
Kamigoryo Shrine
Takano
Japan Baptist Hospital
Hirano Shrine
31
Injo-ji
Hokyo-ji
Jotenkaku Museum
Shokoku-ji
Kyoto University
Ryoanji
Daihoon-ji
Shakuzo-ji
Myoken-ji
Doshisha University
Tanaka
Kyoto Municipal Archaeological Museum
Chion-ji
Kinano
Kitano
Kitano Tenmangu Shrine
Nishijin Textile Center
Imadegawa-dori
Ginkaku-ji
9
Toji-in
Kitano-hakubaicho
Ryuhon-ji
Kyoto Imperial Palace
38
Shibunkaku Art Museum
Yoshida Shrine
Jodoji
10
The Philosopher's Path
Keishun-in
Hazama Tadashi Shrine
Kosho-ji
Honen-in
Myoshin-ji
Shogoin
Yoshida
Kawaramachi-dori
Imadegawa-dori
WACOAL GROUND
Daiser
Hieidaira
Hayao Shrine

HERITAGE SIGHTS OF NORTHERN KYOTO

The crowds begin to thin, the pace becomes more leisurely and it is definitely cooler in the summer months. From Shirakawa-dori, Kyoto's easternmost street, the roads slope uphill and car traffic is limited to local residents. The Eastern Mountains cast their shadows over the district until late morning, allowing moisture-loving ferns and moss to thrive.

In ages past, anywhere east of the Kamo River was considered remote. But beginning in the 17th century, these foothills attracted wealthy residents with a means of transport into the city, as well as artists who coveted isolation for their ateliers. This mix of the estates of the wealthy and successful artists with distinguished taste, bestowed a reputation for refinement on Northern Kyoto.

Top Bundled branches form the brooms used to gently sweep fallen leaves from delicate moss.
Above A single pine needle tops this carefully formed sand cone at Kamigamo Shrine, a World Heritage Site.

Previous spread A temple monk's life consists of the mundane as well as the spiritual.
Above Bronze guardian lions at the Main Hall of Kuramadera.
Left Pagoda at Amida-do Temple at the Buddha Hall of Enryakuji Temple, a World Heritage Site, located atop Mount Hieizan.
Right Black, white and red—nature's gift to the winter visitor.

GINKAKU-JI
THE SILVER PAVILION

Originally an emperor's villa, the Silver Pavilion (Ginkaku-ji) was built as a retreat from the demands of ruling and the intrigues of court politics. During the 14th and 15th centuries, the Ashikaga Shogun Takauji won his throne through betrayal and skill. When his grandson Yoshimasa became Shogun, the clan's position was waning and the country was perched on the verge of several wars. The Shogun, then a mere teenager, had little interest in the intrigues of the court and

left the center of power to take up residence in the northeastern district of Kyoto.

To the detriment of a starving, war-ridden populace, the young Shogun pursued his interest in the fine arts. He came under the tutelage of three artists: Noami, Geiami and Soami, who contributed a great aesthetic legacy of painting, architecture and the tea ceremony.

Yoshimasa's estate, built in 1489, was called the Silver Pavilion, but it remained ungilded, either because of an empty treasury or as an allusion to the soft glow of moonlight on the roof.

Wealth and its implied power was shown in the amount of property one owned then and even today. The magnificent approach to Ginkaku-ji, a World Heritage Site, is a clear display of affluence, with its towering, expertly trimmed hedge above a bamboo fence on a cut stone

base. The three-tiered approach goes way beyond a mere wooden gate to announce the status of its resident. This might be the most impressive entrance to any of Kyoto's ancient villas. The first glimpse of the complex is of the *kare-sansui* sand and rock garden through a large cusped window, an aesthetic tease of the most refined sort for the entrant.

After the Shogun's death, the temple became known as Jisho-ji, Yoshimasu's posthumous

Opposite above A gardener steps back from his work. The wrapped towel on his head makes a handy hat, one often used by laborers.
Opposite below The serene reflection of the Main Hall of Ginkaku-ji, a World Heritage Site.
Top left Three tiers of natural materials—stone, bamboo and hedge—denote an Imperial villa.
Top right The blush of woodwork at sunset.
Above left Schoolchildren crossing the garden's pond.
Above The symmetrical raked sand garden beyond the elegant curve of the cusped window.

Buddhist name. Today, monks practice and reside here, so entrance to the buildings is not permitted, but it is the gardens that attract thousands of visitors a year. The white raked sand and rock garden beside the main pavilion enhances the effect of a moonlight setting, shimmering in the light. Although the dry garden is strictly for viewing, the grounds are traversed with paths that lead to a pond, waterfall and sloping trails that offer numerous views of the grounds.

Lying as it does in the shade of the wooded hills, the Silver Pavilion enjoys a luxurious abundance of different kinds of moss. Unobtrusive flowering plants, such as those used in tea gardens, mostly in soft hues and not too fragrant,

bring a stillness to the complex.

There are two sand cones in the front garden, one suggesting Mount Fuji, or a sacred Buddhist mountain in China. These later additions have been a tantalizing puzzle to many since they were not part of the original design, but they create a focal point of special interest to visitors.

とても邪魔な苔

Opposite above A bridge formed from a single slab of granite.

Opposite below The conical sand dome represents a mountain piercing the surface of the sea.

Center left A less formal stroll garden leads up the foothills of the Eastern Mountains.

Left The sheer elegance of materials and landscaping make a visit to Ginkaku-ji a rewarding aesthetic experience.

Above Various types of moss are labeled for visitors.

Below Slender trunked cypress trees rise from the edge of the stroll garden.

TETSUGAKU-no-MICHI
THE PHILOSOPHER'S PATH

Tetsugaku-no-Michi unfolds with temples, Imperial tombs, tiny shrines, cemeteries, shops and galleries, and, in June, a twinkling host of fireflies.

The cherry tree-lined canal is named for Nishida Kitaro (1870–1945), a Kyoto University professor whose philosophy blended East and West, and whose Zen meditation practice included a daily stroll along this route.

South of the Silver Pavilion, the first temple one meets is Honen-in, founded in 1680. Both entrances are lined with stately pines, and in March the blooms of the bush camellia trees pave the approach in fallen pink petals.

The handsome thatched gate embodies the understated beauty characteristic of Japanese art, as well as the humility and simplicity of life lived according to Buddhist principles. More explicitly, the large stone pillar outside the stone stairway asks that those who partake in spirits or eat flesh refrain from entering, two religious precepts to which Buddhists, strictly speaking, must conform.

Beyond the gate are two raised beds of sand that resemble clouds, waves, a swirling cosmos or flower pedals, depending on the skill of the monk and the eye of the beholder. Because Honen-in houses and trains acolytes, only invited guests may enter the inner temple. But the open areas offer rich rewards in the beauty of the

Above left On the edge of the Eastern Hills flows a canal and an ancient path, beloved of the philosopher Nishida Kitaro.
Above A local resident allows a photo of himself.
Right Autumn colors are set against emerald-like foliage in Japan's mild climate.

grounds, an art gallery and a peaceful setting twittering with birdsong in spring and the whirr of cicadas in late summer.

The next temple, Anraku-ji, only opens on spring weekends when the azaleas bloom. It predates Honen-in, but both temples are associated with the founder of Jodo Buddhism, Honen (1133–1212). Except for the May and June display of floral color, the garden's palette is a wide range of serene greens. The graves of two of Honen disciples, killed after they converted court ladies, lie on the grounds.

The Philosopher's Path passes Otoyo Shrine, founded in 865, with its glorious array of winter camellia and guardian stone rats to Eikan-do at its southern end. Named after its founder, the Main Hall houses one of Kyoto's most unusual images of Amida, standing erect but with its head turned to look behind him. Traces of inset abalone shell can be seen in the black-lacquered pillars.

In spring, billowy clouds of the soft cherry blossoms hover above the path, and in autumn their leaves, tinged with gold, add a lustrous display of nature's art.

Opposite above left Mounds of azalea are about to burst with color at Anraku-ji Temple.
Left The thatched gate of Anraku-ji acts as a symbol of the humility and simplicity of Buddhist life.
Top The fallen petals of multicolored camellia bushes on raked sand within the inner garden of Honen-in.
Above A resident monk dressed for early morning chores.

Top The entrance to Honen-in has two raised beds of sculpted sand, variously interpreted as seascape, coastline, waves, clouds and flowers—depending on the imagination of the creator.
Above Monks follow the path through the towering pines.

SHISENDO
HOUSE OF THE
IMMORTAL POETS

Exceptionally large deciduous trees cast year-round shade on the modest stone walkway to the former villa of poet and calligrapher Ishikawa Jozan (1583–1672). But the unassuming entrance is deceptive. The sloping grounds of Shisendo, now a Soto Zen temple, reveal one of Kyoto's most elegant gardens.

Ishikawa, forced to leave Edo and take the tonsure in 1615, retreated to this site to build his villa and write. It still remains somewhat isolated, one reason why it is so attractive. As one moves past a set of standing folding screens to the villa's veranda, light suddenly pours from an expanse of dazzling white sand. Expertly trimmed azalea bushes enclose the garden's edge, backed by the forested hillside. This is where most visitors sit and enjoy the beauty before them. The only sound, other than whispered conversations and the gentle rustling of bamboo leaves, is a sudden clack as a bamboo tube behind the azalea bushes fills with water, upends and strikes the stone below. This device, called a *shishi-odoshi*, or deer cautioner, is used to scare stray deer or wild boar from entering the garden. Nowadays, the sound recalls a rustic remoteness that vanished long ago.

Left Cell phones and cameras are easily tucked into an *obi*. **Right** Azaleas have been cultivated in Asia for centuries and Shisendo has some splendid examples.

The garden has a lower level, which guests are encouraged to visit. It is only after donning slippers and moving into the garden that the structure's charming moon-viewing tower, an appropriately poetic conceit, can be seen.

The lower level has an aged wisteria arbor of purple and white blossoms in May, along with a few scattered seats that afford a little privacy to visitors.

Ishikawa was a poet and calligrapher, and as a tribute to the literati who lived before him has paintings of the 36 classical poets made by the famous Kano Tan'yu mounted in one of the chambers.

The contrast between the dark interior of the rooms and the sparkling exterior creates a dramatic contrast in the use of light and shadow. The forested hillsides have been incorporated into the landscape, contributing to the secluded atmosphere. Deep pink azaleas set the garden ablaze in spring, maples in autumn and, in winter, the blooms of a particularly large camellia bush bring a minimal splash of color to the landscape palette.

Top left When upturned, the water-loaded length of bamboo tips and strikes stone, sounding a caution to approaching deer.
Top right The reluctant gardener's task.
Above Sculpted azalea bushes are about to transform the garden with color.
Right Irregularly shaped stepping stones in a symmetrical setting, a microcosm of Zen landscaping.

SHUGAKUIN
IMPERIAL
VILLA

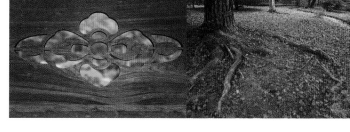

Of the three Imperial villas that require permission to enter, Shugakuin, with its dynamic mountain-backed setting, has the most expansive scenery. Unconstrained by the highly regulated design of most gardens, the scale is as imperial as its designer and first resident, Emperor Gomizuno (1596–1680). The villa was Gomizuno's retreat after he abdicated, but he visited only occasionally, and the fragile and transient appearance of the buildings adds to their preciousness.

An official guide leads visitors along the pathways, pointing out important structures and the poetic references employed to enhance a view. Sophisticated gardening techniques are evident everywhere. In autumn, red and yellow maples emerge from the same trunk, a testimony to the skill of the gardeners to successfully graft different species of trees in order to create such a rich botanical display.

The stone lantern, named the "kimono sleeve," is sometimes referred to as the alligator's mouth, and is an amazingly modern looking ornament considering the villa was built in 1650, an indication of the timelessness of Japanese artistry.

The middle villa was the residence of the Emperor's eighth daughter. Amid its multitude of flowering shrubs is a magnificent spreading pine tree, named "the umbrella pine." Several of the doors in this old residence are painted, some with artisans dyeing *kimono*, others of Gion Festival floats. One of particular interest is of large carp that used to elude the fisherman's net until the famous artist Maruyama Okyo (1733–95) painted nets over them to capture them forever on these wooden doors.

The upper villa was meticulously designed by Gomizuno to incorporate the panorama of forested hills and glistening pond

below, one of Kyoto's greatest examples of "borrowed scenery." The fabulous reconfiguration of nature seems completely natural.

The walk slows as visitors are guided around the shallow, manmade pond, which cools residents during the sultry summer months. A fine example of carpentry and design, "The Bridge of Eternity" rests near the mouth of the pond, donated by an admirer to the Emperor in 1824.

To the south lie the Imperial rice fields, still farmed by local farmers, an elegant combination of the regal and rural nature of Japanese aristocracy.

Opposite above Pebbles set in a *hi-fu-mi* pattern mean: one, two, three as well as "beautiful skin."
Opposite below A blending of architectural styles: Chinese influence brought windows that hinged from above and were kept open with stays, whereas Japanese doors and windows slide open.
Top left Wide placement of garden materials creates a spacious stroll garden.
Top right Terraced rice fields next to the Shugaku-in Imperial Villa begin to ripen. The fields were acquired in 1964, and are leased to local farmers to produce rice for themselves and the Imperial family.
Above left A floral crest.
Above right Brilliant maple carpeting.

SHIMOGAMO AND KAMIGAMO SHRINES

Founded by Kyoto's earliest settlers in the 7th century, the Lower and Upper Kamo Shrines predate the city's role as Imperial capital.

The Kamo clan's tutelary shrines host the annual Hollyhock Festival. Every May, a young woman, appointed to act as Saio, an Imperial priestess, travels by ox-drawn carriage to the World Heritage Sites accompanied by hundreds of attendants in Heian-period court dress, led by a young man on horseback acting as the Imperial messenger. The stately, hours-long procession moves from the Imperial Palace to Shimogamo Shrine, along the Kamo River (named after the clan), and ends at the Kamigamo Shrine. City traffic halts as the plodding oxen pull the wisteria-draped carriage bearing the regally seated, swaying Saio.

Numerous minor shrines are set amidst the extensive wooded park along the heavily shaded paths to Shimogamo. Tadasuno-mori, "The Forest Where Lies are Revealed," was considered a place of judgment, as well as a site that could repel misfortune. The shrine's primeval forests are never cut or pruned, and sections destroyed by fire are left to regenerate naturally.

Kamigamo Shrine in the north, related to Shimogamo Shrine, has expanses of lawn on either side of its approach, which are reserved for equestrian events twice a year. Horsemen in ancient court dress re-enact the travels of a messenger from the Imperial Palace, who rode to the shrines to read the message from the Emperor praising the gods and asking for their continued divine guidance.

Close to the entrance to the shrine grounds is a wooden stall for the Imperial horse, a steed that represents a messenger to the gods. The little wooden plaques sold, and left to hang at shrines, are called *ema*, a votive tablet with a picture of a horse, once a highly desired possession, as well as a means to convey one's written wishes to the gods.

Representing the mountain where the shrine god descended, two sand cones rise in the courtyard. Each is topped with a single pine needle, alluding to the word for "pray," a homonym of "pine" (*matsu*).

Small stone bridges span the stream, the Myojin River, that flows through the shine's precinct and joins the waterway outside the shrine, flowing past the beautiful old residences of generations of shrine priests.

Above far left The heavily wooded approach to Shimogamo Shrine.
Above center left Two sharp claps to catch the gods' ears, a whispered prayer and a bow of thanks.
Above left Maple leaves entangled in slender *shaga* lily leaves.

Above A visitor entering Shimogamo.
Opposite below A single pine needle tops this mound of sand, welcoming the gods to descend to earth.
Below A shrine priest approaches the arched cinnabar-colored bridge at Shimogamo.

DAITOKU-JI
THE TEMPLE OF GREAT VIRTUE

A signboard, now gone, in this complex noted the five desires of mankind that monks in Zen training vow to suppress: wealth, sex, food, pride and sleep. Several times a year, the thwack of a flat wooden stick will resound through the grounds. Sleep and distraction are so tempting during an all-night meditation session that acolytes bow and request the attending monk to administer this sharp stimulus to enhance focus.

Zen temples house Kyoto's great repositories of 16th century art forms, including exquisite tea-rooms with their gardens, utensils, fine calligraphy and brush-and-ink paintings. Set in a residential area, the Daitoku-ji Temple complex is open to the public, but the sub-temples, which contain some of Kyoto's finest *kare-sansui* Zen gardens, require an entrance fee.

Daitoku-ji is a Rinzai sect Zen temple that was established in 1319, and was gradually enlarged under the largess of the wealthy patrons from Sakai City and the famous abbot Ikkyu (1394–1481). Sakai City, in southern Osaka, had many tea enthusiasts, one of whom, Sen-no-Rikyu, later became a leading proponent of this art while living in Kyoto.

When tea first came into wide use, it was imbibed for its medicinal value. As a stimulant, it allowed monks to stay awake during long meditation sessions. Eventually, thanks to the genius of its early practitioners and enthusiasts, the act of making and receiving a cup of tea was codified into a ceremony, further evolving into a spiritual discipline as well as a sophisticated form of entertainment.

Daitoku-ji's main buildings, as with most Zen temples, are constructed on a north–south axis, with all halls facing south. The first major building in this grid is a large cypress-covered gate, the "Imperial Messenger's Gate," and directly north of it is the vermilion Sammon Gate, with a history

that brings into focus two of Japan's most famous men: the warlord Toyotomi Hideyoshi (1537–98) and Sen-no-Rikyu (1511–91), the well-respected tea master from Sakai and a leading connoisseur of the arts connected to tea. Theirs was an entangled relationship of mutual admiration and jealousy. After a strain in their relations, Rikyu ordered

Above Fallen pine needles feel the gentle sweep of the broom.
Right Islands of moss are created in the raked seascape.
Below Moss that has been carefully cleaned of intruding plants.

an image of himself put on the second floor of the gate, knowing that Hideyoshi would pass beneath his image. Hideyoshi did, and upon learning what Rikyu had done, ordered Rikyu to kill himself, bringing an end to the life of one of Japan's great arbiters in the fine arts, and imbuing the gate with a reminder of the whims of a powerful ruler and a man who challenged him.

All of the subtemples within Daitoku-ji are defined by the Zen aesthetics of rustic simplicity and elegant unpretentiousness. The beauty of patina, whether on a mildew-embedded earthen wall, the aging limb of a pine tree propped up by wooden stays, or the fine crackle of glaze in a well-used tea bowl, are testimonies to the richness and lasting beauty of Japanese aesthetic concepts.

Left The simplicity and mystique of the Zen garden.

Right, clockwise from top left The art of frugality—materials are replaced only when necessary. Metal nail covers. A bamboo fence bound with bamboo straps. Blackened by the rain, these pebbles form a glistening border.

Below Visiting temple gardens is a popular date for young couples.

MOUNT HIEI AND ENRYAKU-JI TEMPLE

Traveling up the mountain via cable car or hiking the 1,000-year-old trodden paths to a site which once hosted 3,000 temples often reduces visitors to a silent reverence.

Enryaku-ji, founded in 806, spreads across mountains redolent of cypress and lyrical with birdsong. The three major compounds of this magnificent World Heritage Site—Todo, Saito and Yokawa—attest to Buddhism's place in Japanese history.

Saicho (767–822), the founder of Enryaku-ji, established the Tendai sect of Buddhism upon his return from studies in China. Braving sea travel, he mastered a new language and con-

cepts, and returned to influence the lives and culture of millions.

Imported Buddhism and native Shinto, represented by the Emperor, co-exist, but the abbots of Mount Hiei were proselytizing a foreign faith. Using the belief that evil emanated from the northeast, they assured the Imperial court that the monks' prayers on this northeastern mountain would shield the city from harm. The Emperor accepted that protection, and Enryaku-ji's fortunes flourished. The number of monks grew, as did their power, both religious and military.

In 1571, political boundaries were crossed and the warlord Oda Nobu-

Far left Banners are hung to mark a religious event.
Center left Rising through the thickly forested mountaintop of Mt. Hiei is the roof of the massive Main Hall of Enryaku-ji Temple, a World Heritage Site.
Left A sacred jewel in Jizo's upturned palm.

Left A view of Mount Hiei incorporated into the garden of Shoden-ji Temple, a technique known as *shakkei*.
Bottom Tendai Buddhist priests in richly woven garments.
Opposite below A precise task.

naga burned the temples to the ground and massacred the entire population. In the 17th century, Oda's successor, Hideyoshi, and the Shogun Tokugawa rebuilt the monastery and some sub-temples. Today, a mere 70 remain, but all are glorious testaments to religious devotion and the will to maintain this veritable religious city atop an 824-meter-high mountain.

Immediately inside the Konpon Chudo Hall is an open courtyard, reminiscent of Chinese architectural influence, with two thickets of bamboo that are a symbol of hope that this sect would take root in Japan and grow.

Three lanterns remain eternally lit before an image of Yakushi Nyorai, the Buddha of spiritual and physical healing, in the recessed altar in the interior of the Hall, blackened from centuries of candles lit by petitioners.

Below a coffered ceiling, fine sculpted figures of winged bodhisattvas and paintings decorate the walls in a *tatami* room were visitors and devotees mingle.

The antiquity of the structure and the towering cypress forest that surrounds it impart an austere but serene beauty.

KURAMA VILLAGE

The Keifuku Eizan railroad from Demachi Yanagi offers visitors and local residents one of the city's most scenic rides to this northern village in its comfortable glass-enclosed cars.

This remote area—still inhabited by monkeys, serow (mountain goats), bear and deer—evokes the story of Minamoto no Yoshitsune (1159–89). After rivals killed his family, they spared the young boy on condition that he enter the priesthood at Kurama Temple. He obliged his captors by studying the sutras, but snuck out into the forest at night to meet and be trained by a master swordsman. People point to the split boulders scattered around the mountain as evidence of his prowess with the sword. Although the rifts result when water drips into the rock, children love the legend of this hero, and believe that the mysterious master swordsman was actually a *tengu*, sometimes pictured as a long-nosed, red-faced man and at other times a mythical creature with a bird's beak, as evidenced by all the masks on sale near the station.

Trekkers, pilgrims and tourists disembark from the train at its terminus to begin the ascent up the long stone stairway. There is a cable car but the walk is much more satisfying, for the surrounding forest, with its 100-meter-high cypress trees, imparts a spiritual dimension that is unique to mountaintop temples. Midway up the steps is Yuki Shrine, where visitors pass under the elegant, unadorned cypress roof that covers a divided hall.

Supposedly, centuries ago the shrine's deity arrived in the form

Left Tengu, the long-nosed goblin, a mythical resident of these mountains.
Below far left The mountaintop temple in Kurama resides in a jeweled autumn setting.

Below center The cinnabar railing competes with nature's shades of crimson.
Below The *torii* gate leading up to the temple.
Bottom left The Eizan trainline

from Demachiyanagi Station offers passengers views from both sides of its cars.
Bottom right The conductor's seat along this picturesque mountain track.

of a flaming torch carried from the Imperial Palace. Every October, in one of Kyoto's major fire festivals, the town re-enacts this event. Village men carry enormous torches through the streets to the shrine, sparks scattering in the wind and showering down on to onlookers.

Having repeatedly experienced the destructive power of fire, the mountaintop temple of Kurama

Above The Main Hall atop Mount Kurama.
Below Snow—another layer of beauty.
Right Scarlet lanterns line the approach, visitors ascend on the left and descend on the right.

is made of concrete, but this does not detract from its spiritually imposing atmosphere. The interior is ancient, filled with the fragrance of incense and with Buddhist images that date back to the 10th and 12th centuries.

The sacred flat rock enclosed with straw rope outside the Main Hall is associated with Mao-son, the temple's principal deity. From here, numerous peaks, fading into the misty distance, reaffirm the steep mountainous terrain of Japan as well as the tenacity of devotees in building on these isolated peaks.

Above Pilgrims and trekkers visit Okuno-in, a small sub-temple deep in the mountain.
Above right Rural houses in the village hug the main road.
Right The roots of giant cryptomeria trees are exposed due to centuries of gradual erosion.

A short distance from the Main Hall is a rise entangled with the exposed intertwining roots of massive cypress trees. Although many of Japan's forests have been extensively logged, the slopes of sacred mountains such as Kurama remain primeval. Centuries of slow erosion have exposed the gnarled roots that seem to cling to the mountain. They—along with ferns, wild lilies, bush camellia and moss-carpeted ground—help visitors experience the sanctity with which Japanese regard their mountains and other natural phenomena.

OHARA VILLAGE

The old Saba-kaido (Mackerel Route) curves through the mountains to the Japan Sea coast, starting from the east side of Kyoto and passing through the old farming village of Ohara.

The valley is wide, with roads shaded by cherry trees in spring and rice fields lined with brilliant amaryllis in autumn. Its picturesque appeal attracts many artists to set up their easels and photographers to roam the slopes searching for a drowsy dragonfly or fluttering cherry blossoms against a backdrop of thatched farmhouses and bubbly streams.

The village's remote and bucolic feeling is best represented by Oharame, women in cotton indigo *ikat* who craft and cart small bouquets of home-grown flowers twice monthly to the inner city for family and neighborhood altars.

Ohara is also the home to some very special temples, Sanzen-in being the best known and most visited. Its ancient Amida Hall was first built in 985 and rebuilt in the same style in 1148. It is shaped like an inverted boat to accommodate the immense image of Amida purportedly carved by the temple's founder, Genshin. A hundred years later, two images, Kannon and Seishi, were carved and assembled from blocks of wood and placed on either side of the main image. The walls have traces of paintings that once filled the dark hall with color. The building, which is called Ojo-Gokuraku-in, the Temple of Rebirth in Paradise, and its hushed setting in an expanse of lush moss dappled with sun-

light filtering through the tall cyrptomeria trees, is truly otherworldly.

The monks from Mount Hiei came to Ohara to be trained in *shomyo* or Buddhist chanting. Set out on a shelf in Hosen-in is a set of stones, which, when struck, sound the tones to chant a sutra.

Hosen-in also preserves the bloodied floor planks taken from Fushimi Castle, when, in 1615, hundreds of warriors faithful to the first Tokugawa Shogun, committed mass ritual suicide rather than surrender. Distributed to several temples, the planks at Hosen-in form ceilings so that no foot can ever desecrate the warriors' sacrifice.

Throughout this naturally beautiful valley, tiny vegetable patches are interspersed with rice paddies, produce dries in farmhouse courtyards, persimmons hang from eaves, and hawks soar effortlessly overhead.

Opposite above Whisking up the fallen leaves.
Far left Mountain trails allow for fine views of this valley.
Center left A masterpiece of sculpted sand in Hosen-in.
Left The view from Hosen-in.
Top Among their temple tasks, twice a year monks must corral the fallen leaves.
Above At Hosen-in, a priest explains the origin of the post-battle, blood-smeared ceiling preserved in the temple.

CHAPTER 4
WESTERN
KYOTO

Western Kyoto

0   500m
0   1500ft

N

Sekisui-in
Hachimangu Shrine
Saimyo-ji
162
Dongyo-ji
Jingo-ji
26
Kiyotaki Daigongen
Takao
Isho-ji

Mt. Sawayama
516m

Mt. Momoyama
460m

Shini Por
Josho
Genko-an
Koetsu-ji

Okitayama

Hidari-daimo

Mt. Washiga-mine

Arashiyama Takao Parkway

Shobudani-ike
Pond

Sowanoike
Pond

Haradani Cherry Garden

Mt. Daimonji-
yama

Shuzan Kaido

Kinugasa

Kinkaku-ji Temple
20

Kyoko-chi

Domoto
Museum

Wara-te

Jikishi-an

162

Sampo-ji

Umegahata

Saiju-ji

Yomeibunko

Ryoan-ji Temple
21

Mt. Kinugasa

Ritsumeikan
University

Kitasaga
136

Torii-gata

Daikaku-ji

Osawanoike
Pond

Hirosawaike
Pond

Narutaki

Ninna-ji Temple
22

Ryoanji

Toji-in

Hir
Shri

Kitano

Fukuoji
Shrine

Utano

Ryoanji

Toji-in

Kitano-hakuba

Adashino
Nembutsu-ji

Gio-ji

Seiryo-ji

Yamagoe

Omuro
Ninna-ji

Myoshin-ji

23

Keishun-in

Prefectural
Gymnasium

Takiguchi
-dera

Hokyo-in

Hensho-ji

Narutaki

Keifuku Kitano Line

Myoshin-ji Temple

Taizo-in

129

Nison-in

Rakushisha

Marutamachi-dori

Hanazono

Jojakko-ji

Arashiyama
24

Saga
Arashiyama

Hoju-ji

Tokiwa

Uzumasa

Hanazono

Hokongo-in

JR Sagano Line

Hanazono
University

Enmachi

Ogurayama
Tunnel

Okochi Sanso

Torokko
Arashiyama

Tenryu-ji

Rokuo-in

Kurumazaki

Randensaga

Arisugawa

Toei Movie Land

Koryu-ji

Katabira-no-tsuji

Ukyo Ward Office

131

**Uzumasa-
Yasui**

Tenjin R.

Daihikaku

Arashiyama

Ranzan

Kurumazaki
Shrine

Kyoto Saga
University of Art

Shochiku
Movie Studio

Uzumasa-
Koryuji

Kaiko-no-yashiro

Uzumasa Tenjingawa

Nishioji-Oi

Katsura River

Sagano
25

Uzumasa

Yamanouchi

Sanjo-dori

Keifuku Arashiyama Line

Horin-ji

Arashiyama

133

Nishioji
Sanjo

Iwatayama Monkey Park

Umenomiya Taisha

Mitsibishi Motors

Kyoto University of
Foreign Studies

Sai

29

Shijo-dori

HERITAGE SIGHTS OF WESTERN KYOTO

In the foothills of Kitayama, beyond the northwestern corner of the neat grid that bounded ancient Kyoto, lie large, elegant estates and villas formerly owned by court nobles, two of which are now famous Zen temples. Past them lie the houses and flat open fields of Sagano and

Arashiyama. Over the centuries, these districts were continually destroyed when the Hozu River flooded, entering the city from between the sharp ravine that cuts through the mountains of Arashiyama.

The steeply pitched road north from Sagano continues upward until crossing Togano-o Pass and down into a thickly forested narrow valley and to a temple even older than Kyoto, a hideaway for a monk escaping from the intrigues of the Nara court.

Today, the Takao district is populated by the woodsmen who cut then re-forested the mountainsides with the famous cedars of Kitayama. Sophisticated centers of Buddhist pursuit, ancient villas and fabulous scenery lie at the foot of these.

Previous spread Leaving no footprint behind is one of the secrets of Zen gardening.
Top Moss-encrusted stone figure.
Top right An isle of pine and fallen pine needles.

Left A young, energetic rickshaw driver regales visitors with local lore while whisking them through the narrow byways.
Center right Weary visitors.
Right Dories—shallow-bottomed boats—are available for parties to view the scenery from mid-river.

KINKAKU-JI
THE GOLDEN PAVILION

A thousand years ago, the Emperor's palace sat near the intersection of Senbon Marutamachi. Favored nobles, granted land nearby, established estates within the city. Others, including the Saionji clan, settled in Kitayama, the North Mountains, a rural hilly area north and west of the official Imperial residences, home to deer and wild boar.

In 1397, the Ashikaga Shogun Yoshimitsu purchased the Saionji estate, rebuilt it and lived there in retirement until his death, whereupon it was bequeathed to his son to convert into a Rinzai sect Zen temple.

During the 14th century, Sung Dynasty architecture and painting entranced Japan. Influenced by its opulent style, Yoshimitsu gilded the roof of his Kitayama house in pure gold. The sumptuous yet delicate structure, poised

Opposite The Golden Pavilion reflected in Kyokochi (Mirror Pond).
Top left Topped by a golden phoenix, the pavilion is a masterpiece of 14th century architecture.
Top right A wattle window set within an earthen wall.
Above A shimmering allusion of Amida's Western paradise.
Left A young woman in cotton *yukata* faces the Golden Pavilion upon which a gilded mythical phoenix perched on the roof glimmers in the summer afternoon sun.

one or, occasionally, two stories, this had three. The first floor, built in the Shinden style popular in the Heian period, has a covered dock for boats, which allowed the Shogun to view the scenery from the pond.

The second floor resembled a hall for an image of Amida Buddha, and the third floor, where Yoshimitsu received his special guests, was adorned, Zen temple style, with cusped windows and paneled doors. Destroyed by fire in 1950, an exact replica was built following the well-studied original plans. The seamless integration of architectural styles reflects Yoshimitsu's eclectic tastes, and has secured the villa a distinguished place in Kyoto history.

The garden, too, is a marvel of accumulated styles that reach back a millennium—one formed from aristocratic tastes to that of a disciplined religion. A rock and sand Zen garden features small isles and outcroppings of rock that

Above Completed in 2003, pure gold leaf was used to restore the pavilion.
Opposite Kinkaku-ji on an early winter morning.
Below, from left to right Splashes of color are reflected on the pond by the bright summer *yukata* the women visitors are wearing.
On the grounds of the Golden Pavilion is a collection of Buddhist images around a container into which visitors toss coins while making a wish.
The waterfall pours forth on a stone that represents a carp struggling to swim upstream, a Zen metaphor for the adversities one must face in a lifetime.
The slim five-tiered stone pagoda that represents the five elements of reality, sits on the islet in the Anmintaku Pond, a reservoir of water used to irrigate the garden below.

gracefully on the edge of a reflecting pond, was considered an architectural achievement and its gold an extravagant touch.

But for many Kyotoites today, the deep luster of the re-gilded roof, completed in 2003 with five times the original amount of gold, while impressive is a little unreal and somehow un-Japanese in its ostentation.

The structure of the World Heritage Site was also remarkable. Where most buildings had only

seem to magically expand their boundaries. The stillness of the water guarantees a near perfect reflection of the pavilion, and even on cloudy days is an ingenious feat of landscape perspective. The scene evokes a more tranquil time, when the only sound was the rustle of passing deer or the flutter of a pheasant in the underbrush.

Yoshimitsu was an ardent admirer of aesthetics whose cultural achievements included his patronage of Noh drama and his creation of an academy of fine arts at Shokoku-ji Temple where he assembled a salon of artists and aesthetes interested in painting, ceramics and the performing arts. After his death, the arts connected to this era became known as the Kitayama Culture.

A visit to Kinkaku-ji encompasses more than seeing a gold-gilded building. It represents an opportunity to view an entire period of artistic splendor.

RYOAN-JI
TEMPLE OF THE PEACEFUL DRAGON

This is a Zen garden that immediately captures the eye, often in bewilderment, and then the heart as the viewer matures. It is *the* iconic Zen garden, in many guidebooks as well as Japanese schoolchildren's textbooks, and one of the most photographed and researched plots of real estate in the world.

The rock garden is located within the walls of the temple—a simple setting yet challenging. Some pass through, unimpressed, others cannot leave. Some might note the compact freshness of the space, gain insight into the islands of stone, absorb the pattern of patina on the earthen walls, or feel the agelessness of beauty. All this does not often happen in a single exposure. Ryoan-ji is like a landscaped *koan* puzzle for onlookers to ponder and

wrestle, an opportunity to question what this space reflects within the onlooker's spirit. It is a garden that expands the confined idea of "garden," and continues to reveal a different perspective with each viewing.

Whether you come on a slow day when only the padding of a few feet and the occasional creaking board intrude on your solitude, or when you are mobbed to distraction by a busload of high school visitors, the garden leaves an enduring impression.

A thousand years ago, a Fuji-wara noble owned the estate. In the 15th century, it passed to the Hosokawa family, and when General Hosokawa Katsumoto died in 1477, it became a Rinzai Zen temple, "The Dragon of Peace Temple."

The *kare-sansui* dry sand and rock garden was likely designed after Hosokawa's death, and rebuilt after a fire in the 1790s. A small mock-up of the garden in the foyer notes that the 15 rock and moss groupings may represent isles in the sea, or a tigress swimming with her cubs.

Opposite left The famed rock garden—a study in the contemplative arts.
Opposite above A water basin shaped like an old Chinese coin.
Above A task that takes years to perfect and hours to perform.
Right The final touches.

The explanations are not meant to be definitive, but only to suggest the possibilities that this space could represent.

Whether the frigid air is dusted with snow or the rocks glisten with summer rain, whether graceful cherry branches brush the earthen walls or brilliant autumn leaves float down on to the raked sand, there is never a bad time to visit Ryoan-ji.

The veranda leads to the back of the temple, passing an unusual water basin shaped like a Chinese coin with a square center. Exiting the temple, paths pass a smaller temple pavilion winding through grounds of softly textured moss and on to a small cemetery for temple patrons.

The pond in the outer garden attracts various transient birds and ducks. An arbor of fragrant purple and white wisteria blooms in May; the vivid azalea bushes in late spring, and pastel water lilies in early summer, and in November, the brilliant purple berries of the Japanese Beauty Berry bushes offset a persimmon tree heavy with deep russet fruit. Both gardens, diligently groomed by a large staff, offset the inexplicable yet genuine beauty of the sand and rock garden within.

Below left The ink brush paintings on the sliding doors in the Main Hall.
Below right An arched stone bridge connects to Benten-jima Island in Kyoyochi Pond.
Right The soft covering of snow brings the garden into another aesthetic realm.
Far right A painting of Chinese immortals on the inner sliding doors.

NINNA-JI
THE TEMPLE OF VIRTUOUS HARMONY

Left A bronze image of a bodhisattva.
Right A view from the veranda of the Shinden reveals a palette of greens highlighted with brilliant red maples.
Far right A *monzeki* temple was an Imperial temple and residence of retired emperors. The sumptuous interiors were adorned with gold foil-backed paintings.

On either side of the entrance to the two-story Ninna-ji, constructed in the early 17th century, stand two huge Nio guardian deities. But the history of the temple goes back to 886 when Emperor Uda retired to Omuro Gosho (Omuro Palace), as it was then known, and became its first abbot. The tradition continued. Members of the Imperial family or high-ranking families given the religious rank of abbot headed temples known as *monzeki*. The walls around Ninna-ji, a World Heritage Site, have five white inset lines designating its Imperial rank.

Fire, war and earthquakes have claimed Kyoto's historic buildings repeatedly but ruling authorities have been wise enough to reconstruct and maintain these religious monuments through the centuries. When the Shinden (Main Hall) was destroyed by fire about 130 years ago, it was rebuilt using

1,000-year-old blueprints. The structure retained its open rooms divided by sliding doors, and covered verandas with low railings that link together several other single-story structures.

From the entrance, the visitor is guided through room after room, each opening on to an artfully constructed view. This temple is also the home of the Omuro School of Flower Arranging and large floral arrangements are always on display in the entrance.

The first glimpse of the eastern garden is of a particularly long pine branch framing the main garden beyond. Viewed from the Shinden, the garden reveals a different scene, alluding to a Chinese brush painting and natural shoreline. The sound of the waterfall was purposefully tempered to enhance the tranquil setting.

Ninna-ji belongs to the Shingon sect of Esoteric Buddhism, and the Founder's Hall is dedicated to Kukai, posthumously

known as Kobo Daishi (774–835). This monk and his followers hailed from the island of Shikoku, where 88 temples form a favorite pilgrimage route for Shingon devotees and, more recently, for anyone desiring an arduous trek for personal or spiritual growth.

In honor of Kobo Daishi, Ninna-ji has a miniature pilgrimage path that winds up the mountain behind the complex. It is dotted with 88 small pavilion-like temples where devotees can pray.

Top left Wooden ornamentation.
Top right Vertical slats in a cusped window.
Far left The elaborately tiled roof of the Shinden beyond a blazing red maple.
Left Arched bamboo stays guide visitors through the moss garden.

MYOSHIN-JI

TEMPLE OF THE MERCIFUL HEART

As with Kinkaku-ji and Ryoan-ji, this temple site was once the estate of Heian nobles, Kiyowara Natsuno (782–837) and later the retired Emperor Hanazono (1308–18), before it became a Rinzai sect Zen temple.

Like Kyoto's four other Zen temples, Myoshin-ji lies along a north–south axis in accordance with Chinese temple dictates, with a *sanmon* (Main Gate, 1599), *hatto* (Lecture Hall, 1656), and *hojo* (Abbot's Hall, 1603). Visitors can apply to join a tour of the steam bathhouse and lecture hall, with its Kano Tan'yu ceiling painting of a majestic dragon circling the heavens. Tan'yu painted this mythical creature with the horns of a deer, the mouth of a crocodile, the scaled body of a carp, the talons of a falcon, and glaring eyes that are said to follow visitors everywhere in the hall.

The bathhouse was an interesting introduction into the daily life of a Zen monk. Cleanliness, like clean clothes, was a worldly pleasure monks were required to relinquish. Even heads had to wait shaving and bathing was allowed only on specific days. Until a few hundred

Opposite above The Japanese tearoom combines simplicity with a touch of rusticity: *tatami* flooring, wood and paper doors and earthen walls. The low door at the back is where guests enter, bowing deeply to enter the humbling world of tea.

Opposite below Raked black gravel sweeps around rocks and moss in the Muromachi-era Zen garden at Taizo-in, established in 1404, the oldest subtemple of Myoshin-ji Temple.

Left Three gentle tugs on the wood beam before releasing it to strike the temple bell at Daiho-in.

Top right A crow-topped tile temple roof.

Right Powdered green tea being served on the temple veranda at Daiho-in.

Below The extended branch of a pine bough below an elegant cusped window.

years ago, the ordinary person did not always bathe in a deep tub of hot water, but typically loosened the grime in a steam room, scrubbed with a brush, and then rinsed with cool water.

Within the Myoshin-ji complex are 47 subtemples, the most famous being Taizo-in, the former residence of the painter Kano Motonobu. Viewed from below, the uniquely steep pitch of the grounds resembles a landscape painting complete with a stream flowing around miniature cliffs and boulders. Unlike the more formal Zen *kare-sansui* rock and

sand gardens, Taizo-in's hilly contours and abundant greenery present a much more natural scene. The painstaking diligence necessary to maintain the grounds reflects the life of a Zen monk, since, in addition to sitting and meditating, tireless mundane tasks must be performed until they are perfected.

In the modern garden he designed, Nakane Kinsaku combined large boulders with smooth-shaped mounds of azalea bushes that perfume the May air, adding a sensual dimension to the usually austere Zen garden experience.

ARASHIYAMA
WESTERN KYOTO

Arashiyama, on Kyoto's western edge, is such a popular destination that three train lines serve it. You can even enter the valley from Kameoka City by a more adventurous route plied by the boatmen who pole the Hozu River rapids through the narrow gorge that cleaves the mountains and empties into the placid basin where egrets and herons perch on the weirs in the river watching families in rowboats and floating food stalls arriving from upstream.

Abundant in literary and artistic allusions, Arashiyama means "Storm Mountains," and when mists descend on its peaks, the area is reminiscent of an ancient Chinese ink-and-brush painting. Its iconic landmark is Togetsukyo, "The Moon Crossing Bridge," an irresistible span used as a motif for *kimono* dyers and artists, and a rustic poets' hermitage, Rakushi-sha, with the enchanting name of "The House of the Fallen Persimmon."

The district's small byways are lined with shivering stands of bamboo interspersed with villas,

Opposite above Rowboats for hire.
Opposite below A boatman poles a passenger craft through the still waters of the Oi River, a heavily forested mountain gorge to the west of Kyoto.
Above Togetsu-kyo, the Moon Crossing Bridge that spans the Oi River, is a motif beloved of artists throughout Japan.
Left One charming aspect of Kyoto is its rural areas. This farmer carries her newly harvested Chinese cabbage.
Right The thick thatched roof of Sukiya Zukuri Teahouse at Hogon-in Temple.

homes and farmhouses, while Kyoto's wily resident monkeys claim Mt Iwatayama as home. It is a steep climb but one well worth the effort to have a look at the Japanese macaque, a primate with the northernmost habitant in the world. (Kyoto University maintains two feeding stations in Kyoto and this one is open to the public.)

Across the bridge is Arashi-yama's premier temple, Tenryu-ji, a World Heritage Site. From its establishment in 1339, it was one of the five great Zen temples in the city, with 150 subtemples. Its grounds covered vast tracts of land, but as with many a temple, war, fire and declining finances left it in ruins. The present buildings thus only date back 250 years, but the grounds date back to the Heian era, when they formed the estate of Muso Kokushi (1275–1351), a nobleman, priest and landscape designer. He created a pond and designed the garden's focal point: a grouping of seven vertical rocks inspired by Chinese Sung paintings. Gardening techniques were still developing and the term *shakkei*, a technique whereby background scenery is incorpo-

Above Schoolgirls are entranced to run into a bevy of arriving *maiko*.
Left Taking a spin through the bamboo-lined roads. Lots of young people work the rickshaws, pulling, guiding and chatting with customers all day long.
Above right The Main Hall of Tenryu-ji, a World Heritage Site, diffused with sunlight.
Right, from left Autumn leaves against the roof of the Meditation Hall at Tenryu-ji Temple, bamboo and more bamboo.

rated into the foreground, in this case, the mountain peaks of Arashiyama and Kameyama, was first used here.

Close by is Nonomiya Jinja, where imperial princesses served as shrine maidens, and which also figures in the 1,000-year-old novel, *The Tale of Genji*, when the "Shining Prince" had a rendezvous with Lady Rokujo at the shrine. Romantic connotations abound, now aided by the panoply of love charms available there.

Jojakko-ji is up a long stone stairway, its hillside covered in maple trees and a lovely pagoda near the top of the grounds. Farther along is the temple Nison-in, founded by Emperor Saga in 841, and the site of many old elegant Imperial graves. Remote and quiet, the unadorned gate seems a remarkably humble tribute to the aristocratic spirits who reside within its grounds.

Opposite above The Randen train line serves locals as well as myriads of tourists bound for Arashiyama.
Opposite below Stone figure of a Rakan, a Buddhist saint worthy of receiving respect and offerings.
Above left Rowboats for hire at Y1,400 an hour.
Above Rounded pebbles nestled in star moss.
Left The lyrical sound of water in a lush fall setting.

SAGANO
VILLAGE

Numerous hand-carved stone images sit impassively along the roadsides in this western district, evoking a bygone but palpable religious spirit. The area remains rural, its distance from downtown Kyoto sheltering it from over-development.

The very large temple of Daikaku-ji, originally the 9th century retirement villa of Emperor Saga, lies a little apart from the cluster of sites near the train stations shared by Sagano and Arashiyama. In autumn, the temple pond is the site of moon-viewing activities, when the gentle strum of the Japanese *koto*, a horizontal harp-like instrument, provides a soothing complement to the moon's lustrous reflection.

Long ago, unable to afford a proper burial, the bodies of the dead were left along the nearby foothills. People marked the simple graves with a stone image praying for the repose of that spirit. As the images increased, they were gathered up and placed in Adashino Nebutsu-ji and cared for by the temple's devotees.

Routes out of Kyoto pass through Sagano, where pilgrims and travelers once paused at wayside teahouses for a respite from the journey and weather. Tsutaya, with its large paper lantern and heavy thatched roof, still welcomes passersby in its rustic yet elegant tearooms. The sun never bestows more than a sliver of light on this teahouse, but the penetrating shadows imbue the old structure with a settled beauty that photographers cannot resist.

One large vermilion *torii* gate, the entrance to Atago Shrine, sits astride

the approach at the western end of Sagano. Farther along, the road passes through a tunnel, then descends to the tiny hamlet of Kiyotaki, famous for its waterfall and stunningly beautiful riverside walk to Takao. The second *torii* is at the foot of a steep stone stairway that climbs Kyoto's highest mountain, Mt Atago (924 m). The two and a half hour trek to the top requires sturdy legs and stamina. But hundreds do it weekly, some as exercise and others to win the gods' protection from fire, the bane of a city filled with wood construction.

Above, from left to right A wayside moss-clad Buddhist image. Monks steering their boat in Daikaku-ji pond. Splashing water to keep down the dust at the entrance to Nison-in Temple. A straw hat and mantle left to dry at the rustic cottage in Rakushisha where Basho wrote *Saga Nikki*.
Center, left to right Handicrafts and mementos for visitors to the Sagano area. Cranes fly among stylized clouds in this wood relief on the wall of the Main Hall at Nison-in Temple. Pine trees against gold foil-backed wooden doors.
Opposite below An arched bridge at Gosha Myojin Shrine and Osawa-no-ike pond, said to be the oldest garden pond in Japan, at Daikaku-ji Temple.
Left A revered red pine finds the support it needs to flourish.

Right Tiled roofs emerge from a steep forested valley.
Opposite top left The simple practice of meditation and the orderly placing of sandals form part of a priest's life.
Opposite top right Symmetrical patterns and those of nature are present in this view from Kozan-ji Temple.

TAKAO
VILLAGE

On the far side of the Togano-o mountain pass, the road descends into a narrow valley where the famous Kitayama cedars are grown and harvested. For centuries, man decimated this precious resource. After wide swathes of hillside were lost to the lumber needs of a growing city, erosion triggered landslides and rivers filled with silt and flooded. Eventually, leaders were pressured to implement policies to ensure timber for future generations.

Today, while much of the lumber for house construction is imported, Japanese-grown wood remains a vital part of interior design and lumber warehouses dot the valley.

Takao is also noted for its luxurious growth of maple trees, and in autumn chartered buses fill the area with visitors eager to admire the brilliant red blaze of foliage. Mention of the maples causes Kyotoites to gaze into the distance and smile knowingly.

Within the temple complex of Kozan-ji, a World Heritage Site, is Sekisui-in Hall, a renowned example of 13th century architecture, with its delicate roof line and overall simplicity of design. Up a slight slope in the western part of the complex, shaded by tall cedar trees and moist with moss and lichens, are rows of tea bushes, replanted here, the site of the original plantation brought from China by the monk Eisai in the 13th century.

It is within this isolated hamlet that a disgruntled priest fled the intrigues of the 8th century Nara court to establish Jingo-ji, a temple with many treasured images belonging to the Shingon-shu, the Esoteric sect of Buddhism. The wide stone steps up to the Main Hall are so steep they tempt the climber with visions of cliff-clinging Himalayan retreats.

Within the Main Hall is a pair of enormous hanging scrolls, the Two Worlds Mandala and the Womb Mandala, a National Treasure and an extraordinary work of Buddhist art. Another National Treasure is the statue of the Healing Buddha, which is carved from a single piece of wood.

A visitor may try to break the profound quiet by turning the heavy stone prayer wheel, but the slight grinding sound is swallowed by a vast open courtyard reminiscent of ancient palaces, and evocative of an era that is lost in time.

Above Descending the moss-softened stone stairway at Jingo-ji.
Right After a sudden rain, the veranda at Kozan-ji needs the touch of a dry cloth.

CHAPTER 5
SOUTHERN
KYOTO

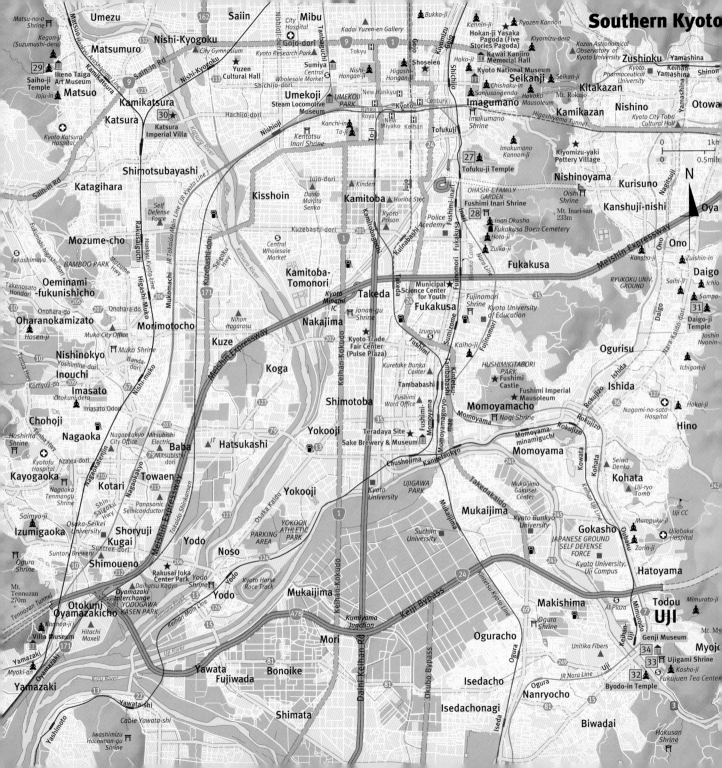

HERITAGE SIGHTS OF SOUTHERN KYOTO

Mountains surround and cradle Kyoto's broad flat plain, where three major rivers, the Hozu, Kamo and Uji, converge to form the Yodo River, which then flows through Osaka to the Inland Sea. When flooding was a seasonal hazard, most buildings rested on higher land or hills, but close enough to

rivers for farming and to facilitate the transport of goods, including produce from the fields that still comprise Kyoto's southern outskirts.

The rivers are now embanked, and the highways and three train lines that carry people and goods have forever altered the character and look of the landscape. Some farmlands and features have disappeared entirely, including the entrance to the ancient capital, Rashomon Gate, which lay a little southwest of where Kyoto Station is now located.

Above Nio, one of the fierce-looking temple guardians at the entrance gate to Daigo-ji.

Previous spread Vermilion tributes to the gods' blessings sought by businesses: a thousand *torii* gates line the pathway up Mt Inari, each bearing the name of the donor on the upward approach.

Top left Sunset reveals the fine carpentry and tile work of a wing of the Phoenix Hall at Byodo-in Temple.
Top right Square stones in billowing mounds of moss, the famous garden designed by Shigemori Mirei at Tofuku-ji Temple.
Left The closing utterance of "un" from a stone guardian dog at Uji-gami Shrine, a World Heritage Site.
Right A tea ceremony guest in the garden of a subtemple at Daigo-ji.

TOFUKU-JI
TEMPLE

Zen was the last major Buddhist sect to enter Japan. By the 13th century, Kyoto was funding the construction of Zen complexes within the capital and, as with Nanzen-ji and Tenryu-ji, near the Eastern and Western Mountains respectively, away from the old established thoroughfares. Tofuku-ji lies at the very south-eastern part of the city.

Zen exerted tremendous influence on calligraphy, the tea ceremony, gardens and architecture, and today's Zen complexes are significant historic repositories for some of Kyoto's finest works of art.

The oldest temple gate in the country, Tofuku-ji's *Sanmon*, is open only in November, when visitors crowd the grounds to view the famous maples. Below the Main Hall, a narrow ravine filled with slender Japanese maples, is one of Kyoto's most photographed autumn sights. The picturesque covered bridge, Tsutenkyo, spans the gorge and leads to one of Tofuku-ji's sub-temples, Kaisan-do. Its garden dramatically presents a well-known garden concept of a

Opposite above and below The renowned *kare-sansui* sand and rock garden of Tofuku-ji, a study in strength and endurance.
Above Visitors photograph the foliage in the deep gorge.
Left Swirling waves of sand flow past the soft mounds of moss.
Right The Heavenly Way Bridge crosses the scarlet scenery of autumn.

tortoise formed by a cluster of rocks and bushes, and a tree as a crane, motifs popularly used to symbolize longevity and fidelity in marriage.

The Hojo, the Abbot's Quarters, was rebuilt in 1890 and its gardens were redone by the famous landscaper Shigemori Mirei (1895–1975), whose work is undisputedly excellent, innovative and exciting.

In 1939, he set out to reintroduce the essence of the Zen garden by borrowing ancient concepts and enlarging on them. He redesigned Tofuku-ji's gardens with innovative verve.

The front garden, almost overpowering with its strong vertical rock grouping within a confined space, challenges viewers to reflect on the designer's intent.

The use of old granite foundation pillars in the side garden to construct a representation of the celestial Big Dipper, was a revolutionary departure from tradition.

Shigemori's most imaginative work, though, is seen in the north garden. Square blocks of granite inset in an undulating blanket of star moss dominate an open grid. In the west, short, highly pruned azalea bushes intersperse with white gravel to define another checkerboard grid. Both gardens are marvels of modern gardening technology and attentive maintenance.

A unique object of interest is the Tosu, the latrine that served residents in ancient times.

The long, narrow wooden and plaster building has open wooden slat windows that allow users to view two raised rows with evenly spaced marked depressions. The discipline of Zen emphasizes simplicity in daily activities, training its acolytes to focus on the immediate, in an attempt to control and eventually free the mind from secular matters. Keeping this building clean was one such task, and it gives modern visitors a glimpse into a lifestyle that enveloped all aspects of a monk's life, even of the lowliest.

Opposite above and middle The art of Zen gardening: patterns that stimulate thoughts of the universe, eternity and transience.

Opposite bottom A pair of wooden *zori* footwear, the kind worn by priests, rests on a gray-slate tiled floor in a sub-temple of Tofuku-ji.

Above left Centuries of honed skills and insightful motives produced these gardens to ignite a different kind of awareness.

Above The rain-drenched hills of moss, or mountains rising from the sea?

Left A departure from the usual rock and sand Zen gardens, the stone checkered moss setting in the Abbot's Quarters enhances the viewers' idea of landscape.

127

FUSHIMI INARI SHRINE

The iconic images of brilliant red *torii* gates along the winding paths of Mt Inari is a visual delight for visitors making the leisurely two-hour walk around the mountain. There is nothing like it in any other city in Japan, perhaps in the world.

Inari Shrine, older than the capital itself, is the tutelary shrine of the Hata family, a clan of Korean origin who owned much of the land in the city. They invited the Emperor to make use of its hunting grounds before offering it to the Imperial court as the new capital. Fertile, with a good supply of wood and water, the land could support a growing population, while its surrounding mountains provided natural defenses. The court moved here in 794, and builders soon made use of the abundant supply of timber to construct Inari Shrine and To-ji Temple.

The main purpose of the shrine was to proffer the gods offerings to assure abundant rice crops. After entering Japan around 300 BCE, this nutritious plant quickly became the basic dietary staple and a key trade commodity.

Rice production, and Inari, are closely associated with foxes, and the shrine is covered with their images on prayer plaques and in paintings. Legend has it that a couple of frisky foxes frolicked in the rice fields, and returned at harvest with a bounty of their own, thus binding the image of the fecund fox to that of a good harvest.

Inari Shrine is covered with prayer plaques in the shape of foxes, for not only did Kyoto's early citizens depend on the crop as food, once rice was fermented and made into *sake*, the gods smiled even more broadly on their devotees, including today's red-faced tipsy visitors to the shrine. Casts of *sake* decorate many of Kyoto's major shrines, and especially here, with the nearby breweries in Fushimi, which are major contributors to the shrine.

The *torii* have the names of patrons on the left side as you ascend, businesses on the right side. Written on the top of the posts are two Chinese characters: *noho*, roughly translated means "appreciative offering."

A climb through the vermilion tunnel is to bask in the sensual glow of centuries of grateful donations, tributes to ongoing life and the spirits.

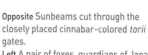

Above Mt Inari is covered with brilliant red *torii*, all given by devotees to the gods that reside in this shrine.
Left Priced according to size, visitors will see hundreds of *torii* on route up the mountain.

Opposite Sunbeams cut through the closely placed cinnabar-colored *torii* gates.
Left A pair of foxes, guardians of Japan's premier crop, hold the sacred key to the rice storehouses in their mouths.
Right A shrine maiden performs a dance to confer the gods' blessings on guests.

SAIHO-JI
THE MOSS TEMPLE

Before Zen reached Japan in the 14th century, other sects preceded it, and one was Jodo. In the 8th century, the garden of Saiho-ji (popularly known as Kokedera), a World Heritage Site, was constructed according to Jodo precepts, a physical embodiment of the spiritual realm, an earthly paradise.

Muso Soseki (1275–1351) was an influential Zen priest and dedicated gardener who believed that landscape could be an effective aid in meditation. Rather than merely enjoying the landscape, he posited that the garden could be an instrument to enlighten. Muso was the first to use the *kare-sansui* dry garden as a spiritual tool. The upper area garden has a cluster of rocks implying a waterfall, with the "flow" of sand swirling away from this grouping. Later, the concept was developed to the point of being almost exclusively thought of

as a characteristic of a Zen garden. Saiho-ji and most later Zen gardens effectively utilize the concept behind the *kare-sansui* as a meditative aid that attempts to ease the grasp of a worldly mind, allowing the student of Zen to reach a more spiritual awareness.

At first, Saiho-ji may seem the antithesis of this sobering rock and sand concept but from the moment a visitor enters, the lush dark green ground covering of moss seeks to soothe and counter a restless mind and lull it into another state by the absolute stillness of its grounds. Muso was also one of the first persons to employ Sung Dynasty paintings of scenery when planning landscape. The emphasis on the insignificance of man, dwarfed by the wonder of nature, proved an attractive precept to employ. The humid

Far left Nestled in a basin, Kyoto is humid year round. This has allowed a proliferation of moss and ferns to take over some gardens as has happened to Saiho-ji, the Moss Garden.
Center left Pathways of irregular shaped stepping stones slow one's pace to impart the timelessness of the scenery.
Left Gardeners with soft-soled *tabi* boots gently gather fallen leaves.
Below The algae-dense pond is a perfect counterpoint to the shades of rich lush green.
Opposite bottom As shadows lengthen, early autumn begins to make its presence felt in Saiho-ji Temple's famous moss garden.

climate of Kyoto assisted his task and the moisture that clings to the moss, trees roots and glistening stones enthralls and comforts.

Visiting Saiho-ji during or after a heavy rain brings out the rich greens of the 40 species of moss in the garden. In the spring, when the trees are budding and the azaleas are in bloom, spots of pink and magenta create lustrous touches of color against the rich verdant backdrop. Maples in autumn add their brilliance to the setting and a greater appreciation of Muso's earthly paradise.

Because of the very large numbers of visitors in previous years, permission to enter is necessary and guests are asked to sit in contemplation before entering the grounds. Those who are skillful with a brush are asked to copy a sutra, but all are asked to respect the religious intent of the temple's priests and creator.

KATSURA IMPERIAL VILLA

Built in 1620 by Prince Toshihito (1579–1629), the villa's garden and buildings are lauded as the quintessence of landscape and architectural design.

Katsura is an intricate tapestry woven of diverse art forms, and created and refined over many years. Appreciating it requires some knowledge of not only Japanese design principles but also of literature and art. The garden paths, for example, reflect Prince Toshihito's literary knowledge by referencing views in famous Chinese and Japanese poems. A miniaturized vista of Amanohashidate is a bow to the long sandbar dotted with tall slender pine trees that lies within his wife's family domain in northern Kyoto.

The Katsura garden is set on a flat piece of land and would seem to make for easy walking, but strolling the garden in *kimono* and *zori* slippers means treading slowly and carefully, especially since the stepping stones are laid at purposefully asymmetrical angles. Forced to look down while stepping, the visitor, on looking up, finds a changed scene, reminiscent of a poem

Left The serene sunlight-dappled interior of the villa offers a garden view from every angle, a masterful merging of architectural and landscaping techniques.

Above Within the building, each opening of the sliding doors sharpens the focal point of the onlooker.

Right A different landscape unfolds from every angle and viewpoint in an eternally refreshing way. Each scene encountered presents the beauty of seasons in different stages of growth, for the gardeners understand how to artfully combine the components of building and landscape.

perhaps or a play, a painting or the passing of a season.

Several words in the Japanese aesthetic lexicon—*wabi*, *sabi* and *yugen*—help explain the underlying concepts. These terms can be applied to the arts, ranging from gardening to painting, flower arrangement to pottery, tea ceremony utensils to architecture. But in gardening, a simple yet elegantly humble example of *wabi* would be how a flower, just com-

Left The rustic and humble yet exquisite thatched gate frames the garden, a conceit that raises anticipation and stimulates the eye.

ing into bloom, triggers an anticipation of pleasure. *Sabi*, the fulfillment of beauty, is felt during the brief pause when that bloom is fully open, but before its petals begin to fall. Another key tenet of garden aesthetics is the use of *yugen*—the sense of mystery and lingering suspense found in a wizened tree trunk or mountain peaks piercing a mist-laden valley.

Another relevant concept is the three levels of formal, semiformal and informal (*shin-gyo-so*). A straight path of rather equally sized and evenly placed stones is regarded as formal, while asymmetrically placed, odd-shaped stones are the least formal. Japanese recognize and appreciate this delineation. Katsura's 1,716 stones, all deliberately positioned on this spectrum of formality, are designed to provoke thoughtful aesthetic pleasure.

Visitors may not enter the buildings, architectural masterpieces whose layout reflects the aristocratic estates of the Heian age that ended 400 years before Katsura was built. Tools had greatly advanced in the inter-

Top right As natural as the gardens may appear, maintenance requires a great number of attentive caretakers.
Above Visitors must step carefully on the irregular stepping stones as they approach the moss-lined earthen and wooden bridge and the hall beyond.

Opposite above left The exposed under-ceiling of the garden pavilion.
Opposite above right A simple woven wattle window and shades of patina in the earthern walls, offset the symmetry of rectangular doors and square paper windows.

Bottom left The reflecting pond extends the scenery from a shoreline of smooth pebbles and the placement of outcroppings of rocks.

Bottom right The low wooden door is the entrance to the tearoom, a study of paper, bamboo and soft earthen walls.

vening centuries and carpenters used rare woods to create enduring, highly detailed and individualized designs. Alcoves display staggered shelves, beams have well-fashioned nail covers and the eaves of each building sit at different levels to create a cascading effect.

A Western villa is usually at its best when approached from the front. But Katsura's entrance is set at a diagonal, so that if viewed from above, the modular rooms of the building complex form a staggered V-shape. This angle allows greater inclusion of garden views to delight the resident and visitor, a complete integration of architecture and landscape.

DAIGO-JI
TEMPLE

Two major sections comprise the temple complex, a World Heritage Site: Shimo-daigo at the foot of the mountain, and Kami-daigo an hour's walk to the top. Both levels of the complex are noted for their magnificent structures.

Founded in the 9th century as an imperial temple, Daigo fell into ruins during the mid-15th century Onin Wars and was restored by the 16th century warlord Hideyoshi, the first person to unite the country politically. He is known for his ruthless military forays but also for his aesthetic pleasures, which included an influential enthusiasm for the tea ceremony, which enveloped all attendant arts—calligraphy, architecture and tea utensils, be they made of paper, bamboo, wood, iron or more precious metals—as well as gardens.

The Sambo-in subtemple, with its opulent garden, is especially representative of the warlord's taste and fortunes. A commoner, Hideyoshi remained a man of the people and hosted massive public events at Daigo-ji, including cherry blossom viewings. Even today, the crowds flock to enjoy the trees in April.

Hideyoshi rebuilt Sambo-in, founded 400 years earlier, in 1595. The garden contains over 700 stones, some gifts from those currying favor, others purchased at unthinkable expense, a display of power, force and subservience. The Heian period *shinden*-style architecture of the building seems ethereal, even indifferent to the bravado of the massed rocks in the garden. A meandering stream flows beneath the veranda at one section, countering the heaviness of the garden.

On the main grounds of the lower level is Kyoto's oldest five-tiered wooden pagoda (951), the second oldest such structure in Japan, and

Opposite Illuminated in the morning sun, a vermilion lacquered arched bridge leads to the Bentendo Hall in the lower precinct of Shimo-Daigo-ji Temple.
Left Meandering streams are an essential part of gardens, supplying thirsty moss with moisture and opening new vistas with each crook in the path.
Below left Monks at work at the entrance to their school, Denpo Gakuin at Daigo-ji.
Below Daigo-ji is famed for its hanging cherry trees, planted by the warlord Hideyoshi in 1598. The petals open and appreciative crowds descend, even after 400 years.
Bottom Japan's most famous warlord, Toyotomi Hideyoshi, was gifted with hundreds of rocks and boulders as signs of allegiance by the lesser lords of the domain, all of which were carefully placed within the Teien Garden of Sambo-in.

farther to the east is the approach to Upper Daigo, marked by Nyonin-do, built as a worship hall for women. Considered impure, females were barred from ascending sacred mountains. Today, however, the tinkling bells attached to pilgrims adorn both sexes as they climb to Kannon Hall, the eleventh stop on Western Japan's Thirty-three Bod-hisattva of Mercy pilgrimage.

The buildings at the top of Mt Daigo are impressive structures, especially considering the labor it must have required in 1121 to con-struct the Yakushi-do Hall, a National Treasure. The image of the Yakushi Nyorai (the Healing Buddha) within dates back to 907. The grounds are forested, the slopes filled with flowering trees.

BYODO-IN
TEMPLE OF THE
PHOENIX HALL

Below As a juxtaposition to the antiquity of the site, a low sleek wooden platform of minimalist design allows visitors to rest and view the landscaped grounds. Below right An image of a celestial figure is on display in Byodo-in so that visitors may appreciate the intricacy of the design.

Top Housing an immense image of Amida Buddha, the ancient temple of Byodo-in seems to take winged flight. The wooden structure is one of the oldest of its kind in the world, unique in its joinery and design. Above Women admire the artifacts in a shop just outside the entrance to Byodo-in. Above center The front gate, bolted shut for the day.

Like the phoenixes atop it, the graceful architecture of the Byodo-in Temple seems about to take winged flight. Within the Main Hall of the World Heritage Site is an image of the compassionate Amida, the Buddha of the Pure Land, believed to save all who invoke his name.

The Pure Land sect gained popularity in the late Heian period (894–1195), when Kyoto's sophisticated Imperial court supported wide ranging cultural growth. The era produced the world's first novel, *Tales of Genji*; a broad expansion of an indigenous alphabet; and the adoption of many cul-

tural imports from China's 6th century Tang Dynasty. The legacy of Heian's artists, carpenters and sculptors inspired their counterparts centuries later to recapture the glory of this extraordinary era in such temples as Katsura Rikyu and Kinkaku-ji.

Fujiwara Michinaga (966–1027), a court noble, bequeathed his villa to his son Yorimichi (922–1074), Regent to the Emperor, who completed the Phoenix Hall in 1060. Only one story high, the struts and elaborate eaves create an illusion of height that is intensified by their reflection in a pebble-bordered pond. Originally, the building was brightly painted, with sumptuous use of mother-of-pearl and lustrous black lacquer. Celestial bodhisattva bearing ancient musical instruments float through the stylized clouds near the gold-leafed image of Amida seated high within the hall, calmly gazing down upon his worshippers, an image created by the sculptor Jocho (d. 1057).

A new museum on the site has a video showing a replica of the original hall in vibrant colors that may seem unreal, almost gaudy, to modern visitors. Accustomed to equating the patina of time with Japanese taste, modern visitors tend to forget that to 11th century sensibilities the building and its interior portrayed the ethereal beauty of a promised paradise and the presence of a powerful deity.

UJIGAMI SHRINE AND THE GENJI MUSEUM

Far left Boat moorings along the river.
Left The Main Hall of Ujigami Shrine, the oldest wooden shrine building in Japan, dated at around 1060.
Opposite Afloat on the Uji River, one of Kyoto's main rivers, flowing from Lake Biwa to Osaka, during the glorious cherry blossom season.

Uji, a town evocative of romantic longings and unrequited love, has a special place in ancient literature.

The town lies a 30 minute train ride south of Kyoto. The walls of the Keihan train station are inset with displays of tea ceremony utensils, because Uji is an area renowned for one of Japan's foremost restorative beverages, green tea. The undulating rows of dense bushes that sweep up and over the surrounding hillsides yield an aromatic tea with the smoothness of fine silk.

Uji's main street is lined with teashops that exhibit old grinding stones and clay jars, which were once filled with the newly picked leaves and proudly carried each year to the Imperial court.

The greatest activity seems to come from the wide and surprisingly vigorous passage of the Uji River as it rushes under the Uji Bridge, first built in 646 and reconstructed many times since then. The mists that rose above the tumbling waters of the river, an important crossing between Nara and Kyoto, appealed to courtiers who established handsome villas along its banks.

Uji also is well known as a setting for the world's first novel, *The Tale of Genji*, written by Murasaki Shikibu (c. 1000). Although Lady Murasaki's hero, "the shining prince," was the son of an emperor, his mother was a low-ranking court lady. Nonetheless, Genji, a handsome courtier and a fine poet, was alluringly sensitive to the dreams of highborn court ladies. The rustling of a silk garment, the subtle fragrance of an incense-infused robe, and the delicate calligraphy of a message brushed on pastel paper, would set the amorous prince in search of yet another romance. The midnight trysts in the story reveal a sophisticated society, entwined by romantic longings that still fill the hearts and dreams of many modern Japanese.

A short walk from Uji Bridge is the country's oldest wooden Shinto structure. Uji Shrine (1060), comprising three small shrines, is so small and unobtrusive that sightseers would often overlook it before it was designated a World Heritage Site. The unadorned cypress structure and the techniques used reflect the construction of the equally old Byodo-in.

Ancient stone-lined culverts line nearby pathways, so that the sound of flowing water accents the gentility that Uji modestly embodies.

Above A twisted straw rope and paper cuttings denote a sacred object, in this case a large rock on the shrine grounds. Loose stones have been tossed with a prayer. Those that stay on the mound will be granted.
Left A twilight view of the statue of noblewoman Murasaki Shikibu, the author of *The Tale of Genji*, published in the early 11th century and considered by many to be the world's first novel. In the background is the Uji Bridge over the Uji River. Uji was the setting of the later chapters, and the place most associated with the book.

BIBLIOGRAPHY

Barrow, John D., *The Artful Universe*, Oxford University Press, 1995.

Castile, Rand, *The Way of Tea*, Weatherhill, 1971.

Clancy, Judith, *Exploring Kyoto*, Stone Bridge Press, 2008.

Fieve, Nicolas and Waley, Paul (eds), *Japanese Capitals in Historical Perspective*, Routledge Curzon, 2003.

Fontein, Jan and Hickman, Money, L., *Zen Painting and Calligraphy*, Museum of Fine Arts, Boston, 1970.

Ishige, Naomichi, *The History and Culture of Japanese Food*, Kegan Paul, 2001.

Keane, Marc P., *Japanese Garden Design*, Charles E. Tuttle, 1996.

Kinoshita, June and Palevsky, Nicholas, *Gateway to Japan*, Kodansha, 1990.

Mertz, Mechtild, *Wood and Traditional Woodworking in Japan*, Kaiseisha Press, 2011.

Nishi, Kazuo and Kazuo, Hozumi, *What is Japanese Architecture?*, Kodansha, 1985.

Richie, Donald, *A Tractate on Japanese Aesthetics*, Stone Bridge Press, 2007.

Richie, Donald and Georges, Alexandre, *The Temples of Kyoto*, Charles E. Tuttle, 1995.

Sasaki, Rither Fuller (ed. Thomas Kirchner), *The Record of Linji*, University of Hawai'i Press, 2008.

Seike, Kiyosi, *The Art of Japanese Joinery*, Weatherhill, 2007.

Shiffert, Edith, *The Light Comes Slowly*, Katsura Press, 1997.

Treib, Marc and Herman, Ron, *The Guide to the Gardens of Kyoto*, Shufunotomo, 1993.

GLOSSARY

aware An aesthetic term meaning compassion or pathos when describing a deeply moving scene or piece of literature.

Buddhism A religion originating in India and entering Japan via China in the sixth century.

cha-no-yu The art of the tea ceremony during which a traditional sweet is served to a guest followed by a bowl of whisked powdered green tea.

chaji A four-hour long tea ceremony in which both thin and thick teas are served along with a light meal.

-cho Denotes a district within the city.

-dori Denotes a street.

fusuma A sliding wood lattice screen covered with an opaque paper panel often decorated with paintings.

gawa/kawa River.

geiko The preferred term for *geisha* in Kyoto.

genkan An entrance to a house where shoes are removed.

geta Raised wooden thong

footwear, worn in summer without *tabi* socks.

-in Denotes a subtemple.

-ji Denotes a temple.

kaiseki Elegant traditional cuisine served in many courses.

kami The gods and spirits of the animist and Shinto pantheon.

kare-sansui A dry rock and sand garden found in many Zen temples.

kimono Used to refer to traditional Japanese clothing.

kinu Silk; when paired with *tofu*, a silky smooth soybean curd product.

komainu The guardian dogs

that are often paired in front of shrines, one with an open mouth, the other closed.

kyoyaki The elegant ceramics produced in the Kiyomizu area of Kyoto.

kyo-yasai Vegetables grown in the Kyoto district.

maiko A young woman studying the traditional performing arts in the *geiko* district of Gion.

mama-charin A sturdy bicycle with seats attached to the back and sometimes front handlebars, used by young mothers to transport their toddlers around town.

matcha Powdered green tea.

miyabi An aesthetic term that indicates a playful elegance.

miyadaiku Specially trained

temple carpenters.

mochi A special type of glutinous rice pounded into round-shaped "cakes".

momen Cotton; when paired with *tofu*, it refers to a heartier, rougher soy bean curd product.

moritsuke The attractive arrangement of food that contrasts color, texture and shapes in one serving.

Noh A form of drama with a spoken libretto and drum and flute accompaniment.

noren curtain-like hanging panels of fabric above shop doorways.

obi A woven silk sash that secures the *kimono*.

ochaya Establishments which offer *geiko* and *maiko* performances; literally a teahouse.

okunomiyaki A wheat-based pancake-like concoction with vegetables, topped with bonito fish flakes and a sweet date-based sauce.

osechi Specialized Japanese cuisine only served during the New Year, originally mostly vegetarian but nowadays with meat and fish products.

pagoda A multi-tiered structure in temple complexes that houses Buddhist relics.

raku The name of a family of well-known Kyoto potters and a form of soft-fired pottery.

sabi An aesthetic term that means the aged beauty of an object.

shakkei Borrowed scenery, a gardening concept that extends and includes the scenery beyond the garden proper.

shamisen A three-stringed banjo-like instrument.

shibui An aesthetic term that means an understated and subtle elegance.

shichimi-togarashi A spicy condiment.

Shinto Native Japanese religion.

Shogun Warlord.

shoji A thin, almost transparent paper used to cover wooden lattice doors and windows.

shomyo Buddhist chanting.

shrine A designated space wherein one can commune with the Shinto gods.

tabi Socks; an ankle-high foot covering which separates the big toe from the others and is worn with *zori* footwear.

tatami Thick rectangular woven covered reed mats used as flooring.

temple A structure that houses Buddhist images and where Buddhist ceremonies are held.

tofu Soy bean curd.

torii The gate to a Shinto shrine, usually constructed

of two horizontal posts and two vertical beams.

uguisu-bari The sound resembling a bush warbler that wood planks emit when trod upon.

wabi An aesthetic term that means beautiful rusticity.

yama Mountain.

yatsuhashi A cinnamon-based curved confectionary.

yuba The skimmed surface of boiled soy beans hung on sheets and sold fresh or in dried curls.

yugen An aesthetic term that means a mysterious beauty that evokes a profound feeling in the viewer.

Zen A sect of Buddhism; that entered Japan in the 12th century and believes that the world and self are illusions.

zori Thong footwear for men and women.

DEDICATIONS AND ACKNOWLEDGMENTS

Dedicated to Eric Oey, for sharing his insights on publishing, and to Judith Clancy, for imparting her wisdom about all things Kyoto.

Heartfelt thanks to June Chong, Chan Sow Yun, Noor Azlina Yunus, Yuichi Kurakami, Yuri Yanagisawa, Takuji Yanagisawa, Tomoyo Yasuda and family, Yoko Yamada, Shiro Nakane, Donald Richie, Mira Locher, Katharine Markulin Hama, Sekiko Yamade, Katsuji Yamade, Hakusa Sonso, Ryokan Rikiya, Julia Nolet, Teiko Seki, Kathryn Gremley, Dennis "Bones" Carpenter, Deborah Collier, Rebecca Stockwell, Sarah Moon, and Michael Gramlow for their kindest support and invaluable assistance.

Ben Simmons, photographer

Writing about Kyoto's major temples and shrines has been an overwhelming task and a joy. I could not have done it without the contributions of people who, over centuries, have documented, protected, preserved and cherished this city's architectural and cultural traditions and treasures. I wish to dedicate this book to them.

Ben Simmon's perceptive photography forms the foundation of the written text. His skill and vision expand the eye and imagination, bringing new life to aspects of Kyoto which contribute to its beauty and well-deserved acclaim.

Appreciative thanks to tea and culinary experts Gary Callwaller and Joseph Justice for their advice on *kaiseki* cuisine.

Catherine Ludvik, a specialist in Japanese religions, patiently answered questions I had about Buddhism, and Thomas Kichner graciously shared his inestimable knowledge as a Zen monk.

Dendrochronologist Takumi Mitsutani provided constructive information on Ujigami Shrine.

Insightful initial editing by Terry J. Allen, a former resident and potter in Japan and now a US-based journalist, gave the text freshness and precision.

Lastly, a word of thanks to editorial supervisor June Chong, who helped me organize years of work into a tribute to the city I love, and which has been my home for 40 years.

Judith Clancy, author

Page 142 above Texting takes preference, even in front of the Honden Main Hall at Higashi-Honganji Temple, a World Heritage Site.
Page 142 below An ancient priestly chore in an ancient shrine.
Page 143 above Vendors clad in traditional wear take a break.
Page 143 below Young women dressed for the afternoon as *maiko* take each other's photos.
Left A boy from a private school totally captivated by a book.
Back endpaper The garden at Tofuku-ji, a perfect synthesis of symmetry and asymmetry.

Published by Tuttle Publishing, an imprint of Periplus Editions (HK) Ltd
www.tuttlepublishing.com

Text © 2019 Periplus Edition (HK) Ltd.
Photos © 2019 Ben Simmons

ISBN: 978-4-8053-1540-8
ISBN: 978-4-8053-1892-8 (for sale in Japan only)
(Revised and expanded edition. Previously published under ISBN 978-4-8053-0978-0)

Distributed by
North America, Latin America & Europe
Tuttle Publishing
364 Innovation Drive, North Clarendon, VT 05759 9436 USA
Tel: 1 (802) 773-8930
Fax: 1 (802) 773-6993
info@tuttlepublishing.com
www.tuttlepublishing.com

Japan
Tuttle Publishing
Yaekari Building, 3rd Floor
5-4-12 Osaki, Shinagawa-ku, Tokyo 141-0032
Tel: (81) 3 5437-0171
Fax: (81) 3 5437-0755
sales@tuttle.co.jp
www.tuttle.co.jp

Asia Pacific
Berkeley Books Pte Ltd
3 Kallang Sector, #04-01, Singapore 349278
Tel: (65) 67412178
Fax: (65) 67412179
inquiries@periplus.com.sg
www.tuttlepublishing.com

27 26 25 24   10 9 8 7 6 5 4 3 2

Printed in China   2405EP

TUTTLE PUBLISHING® is a registered trademark of Tuttle Publishing,
a division of Periplus Editions (HK) Ltd.

"Books to Span the East and West"

Tuttle Publishing was founded in 1832 in the small New England town of Rutland, Vermont (USA). Our core values remain as strong today as they were then—to publish best-in-class books which bring people together one page at a time. In 1948, we established a publishing outpost in Japan—and Tuttle is now a leader in publishing English-language books about the arts, languages and cultures of Asia. The world has become a much smaller place today and Asia's economic and cultural influence has grown. Yet the need for meaningful dialogue and information about this diverse region has never been greater. Over the past seven decades, Tuttle has published thousands of books on subjects ranging from martial arts and paper crafts to language learning and literature—and our talented authors, illustrators, designers and photographers have won many prestigious awards. We welcome you to explore the wealth of information available on Asia at **www.tuttlepublishing.com.**